GOOD
FOOD

BY DOROTHY LARA-BRAUD   FOREWORD BY DR. ALVIN EDEN

INTRODUCTION BY NUTRITIONIST ALEXIS M. BECK

KIDS

DESIGNED BY BARRY L.S. MIRENBURG

LOVE

PUBLISHED BY QUICK FOX, NEW YORK

D1608556

For Nikki Johnstone and Kathryn Leigh Rensenbrink

Acknowledgments: The following people have contributed recipes, and in many instances a great deal of enthusiasm, to this book. We are grateful to Ruth Flaxman, Angie Vogel, Margrit Jones, Judy Weihe, Bernice Vogel, Carole Snyder, John and Judy Flaxman, Lillian Taylor, Josephine Torre, Pat Bryan, Emma Howard, Astrid Antikainen, Martha Man, Joan Dolsay, Ruth Sisco, Debbie Besemer, Jo Janke, Fern Emma Pruiksma, Maryann Vermeulen, Barbara Higby, Marian Allman, Edna Christensen, Marie Den Herder, Anna Dykstra, Sherry Wilkins, Betty Schaaf, Jackie Hugg, Bertha Van Schepen, Pauline Nyland, Marie Intveld, Ellen Faber, Wilma Oliphant, Sherry Wilkins, Olga Struyk, Marion Dob, and Nell Bruinooge.

We would also like to thank Dr. Alvin Eden, associate clinical professor of pediatrics at New York University School of Medicine and director of the Department of Pediatrics of Wyckoff Heights Hospital in Brooklyn, New York. Dr. Eden is the author of many articles and several books, the latest entitled *Dr. Eden's Diet and Nutrition Program for Children.* Also of enormous help has been Alexis Beck, the noted Boston-based nutrition consultant and former director of nutrition services for the Harvard Community Health Plan. Ms. Beck contributed the nutrition notes and charts at the bottom of each recipe.

Copyright © Quick Fox, 1980
All rights reserved.
Printed in Japan.
International Standard Book Number: 0-8256-3199-8
Library of Congress Catalog Card Number: 80-51627
No part of this book may be reproduced or transmitted in any form or by any means, electronic or mechanical, including photocopying, without permission in writing from the publisher: Quick Fox, 33 West 60th Street, New York 10023.

In Great Britain: Book Sales Ltd., 78 Newman Street, London W1P 3LA.
In Canada: Gage Trade Publishing, P.O. Box 5000, 164 Commander Blvd., Agincourt, Ontario M1S 3C7.

Book and cover designed by Barry L. S. Mirenburg
Assistant: David Nehila
Studio photography by David Frazier
Styling: Jamie Simpson

"What are your kids' favorite dishes?"

That was the question posed to countless mothers—in person, by mail, by phone. That was the question that prompted some of the funniest conversations I ever hope to have. Mothers, kids, and food are one of the basic triangles around which important dramas spin daily, very often having to do with what the mother thinks is "good for you" and what the child thinks "tastes good." Those two opinions are often firmly held and, equally as often, in conflict. Hence, the drama. How does it get resolved? These are the impressions that stand out most clearly after talking to so many mothers:

1. Almost all of the mothers recited, by memory, from three to six recipes which they use again, and again, year in and year out. They are the few dishes that have, through a process of creative compromise, achieved the double rank of being both "a favorite" with the kids and "good for you" with the mother.

2. Repetition is no problem with the kids! A child's favorite is like a security blanket or favorite toy: Familiarity is an added charm. But these mothers all thought a collection of favorites that are also nourishing would be a godsend.

3. Children tend to be very conservative about what they eat, and they do not like to experiment. They can be rigidly authoritarian about what they will or will not try, and not necessarily reasonable. There is Jenny, for example, who shudders at the word *egg*. On principle! Her mother came up with a recipe called "Bird's Nest" (see Breakfasts), which is nothing more than a fried egg dropped into a hole in a piece of brown bread. Jenny eats a Bird's Nest every other morning. Happily. "She isn't eating an egg, you see," her mother sighs, "she's eating a picture."

4. The last impression is this: Mothers are still the genuinely nicest human beings there are. The sharing and giving with their small ones carried over through me to your children. This book is their gift.

—Dorothy Lara-Braud

When should a pediatrician write a foreword to a cookbook? Only when the cookbook is written for children and only when the recipes in it are well-balanced and nutritious. If the recipes are also not too high in sugar, salt, and calories, a pediatrician can be even happier to participate.

Dorothy Lara-Braud's book, *Good Foods Kids Love*, by and large meets these criteria and therefore I am pleased to write this introduction.

Despite the abundance and availability of nutritious, healthy foods in the United States, many of our children are growing up on diets that are hazardous to their health and general well-being. Our Western-type diet is not only too high in calories, sugar, and salt, but also in saturated fats and cholesterol. Too many of us, both adults and children, eat too much red meat, too many eggs, and excessive amounts of butter and cream. As a doctor who is interested in preventing illness, I personally recommend that all children be put on the so-called protein diet, which is lower in saturated fats and cholesterol. This kind of diet includes more poultry, veal, and fish and less of the red meats such as beef and pork. I also recommend that children eat no more than three to four eggs per week and advocate the use of corn oil margarine rather than butter whenever possible.

Childhood obesity has reached epidemic proportions. It is now estimated that at least 30 percent of our youngsters are too fat, a national disgrace. The evidence is very clear that the longer a child remains overweight the more likely it is that he or she will always be overweight and have to fight obesity throughout life. Ingrained in our culture is the association of slimness and trimness with beauty. Fat school-age children and adolescents are ridiculed, persecuted, and teased by their peers; they surely must suffer emotional and psychological trauma because of their extra pounds. As a result, many overweight children grow up with negative feelings about their own bodies and develop disturbed and sometimes distorted images of themselves. This inevitably leads to a lowering of their self-esteem and self-confidence. True emotional stability is very difficult to achieve without first developing a positive body image. Those parents who overfeed their children must keep this in mind and change their attitudes about food.

Besides the extra calories, a great many children eat foods too high in both sugar and salt content. The association of high sugar diets and dental decay is well known. What is less well known but probably even more important is the fact that a high sugar intake helps raise the blood fat levels. Since there is a clear and definite correlation between high blood fat levels and the development of atherosclerosis (hardening of the arteries) and all its serious cardiovascular consequences, parents would do well to reduce the sugar intake of their children. In the last few years we have also learned that an appreciable number of school-age children suffer from high blood pressure. Although excessive salt will not by itself cause hypertension, elevated blood pressure can be lowered simply by reducing the daily salt intake. The most frequent single cause of high blood pressure in children, however, is obesity. The great majority of children who are found to have hypertension can be effectively treated by slimming them down and at the same time reducing their daily salt intake.

Our current faulty feeding practices have also led to a very high incidence of iron deficiency in children. A recent preschool nutrition survey found that between 30 and 40 percent of one- and two-year-olds in middle and upper socioeconomic families and between 50 and 60 percent in lower socioeconomic families are iron-deficient. Other studies have shown that at least 50 percent of all adolescent girls suffer from some degree of iron deficiency. Since we now know that insufficient iron in the body can lead to many serious health problems, including behavioral abnormalities, fatigue, anemia, and gastrointestinal symptoms, the magnitude of this problem cannot be underestimated. School-agers and adolescents seldom sit down to eat a well-balanced, nutritious meal. Rather, they eat on the run, usually consuming a junk food diet that is high in carbohydrates and calories and too low in protein and iron. This results in a form of malnutrition even though the child may actually be overweight. Foods that are particularly high in iron content are liver and other meats, eggs, whole grains, dried beans, peas, and nuts, and parents should encourage their children to eat these foods.

In our society a child is usually regarded as healthy if he or she is properly immunized and free of any specific disease. As a pediatrician, let me tell you that nothing could be further from the truth. What we should be asking is whether or not our children can meet their daily tasks, physical activities, and sudden emergencies with enthusiasm, strength, vigor, and coordination, and without tiring too soon. If a child does not have sufficient amounts of energy, I believe that child is just as unhealthy as if suffering from a particular illness.

The important point that all parents must remember is that children learn by example. If proper eating patterns are established early in life it is much more likely that those children will grow up continuing to eat the same way. If children are exposed to a varied, well-balanced, palatable, nutritious diet they will surely learn to enjoy eating that way. Nobody is born a "sugar freak" or a "salt craver." However, if small babies are offered excessively sweetened or salted foods they very quickly learn to enjoy that type of diet and it will be very difficult to reduce the salt and sugar intakes later in life. Similarly, if children are offered a diet rich in fruits and vegetables and with fewer calorie-laden, nonnutritious snacks and desserts, their chances of growing up slim and healthy, with normal blood pressure and lowered risk of atherosclerosis, will be increased.

Dorothy Lara-Braud is to be commended for offering parents imaginative and healthy recipes for their children. Parents who give their children a well-balanced, nutritious diet using the recipes from *Good Foods Kids Love* will help their children grow up healthier and happier.

—Dr. Alvin Eden

Scientific evidence points to the strong influence of childhood food experiences on how we eat as adults. Food preferences, food habits—the healthful and indulgent alike—our overall attitudes toward food and eating, and yes, body size, may have their roots planted in our first bites and our early family environment. An understanding of the factors involved in feeding a child nutritiously may be essential to the establishment of sound eating habits.

With the intention of establishing a national standard, the United States Dietary Guidelines were developed by the departments of Agriculture (USDA) and the former Health, Education, and Welfare (HEW). Emphasizing disease prevention and health promotion, the Guidelines may well be one of the more significant and far-reaching achievements of the last decade; they could form the foundation of a long-sought-after national nutrition policy.

The Guidelines are basic. They encourage our return to the simple dietary objectives of variety, balance, and moderation.

Specifically, the Guidelines ask us to:
1. Eat a variety of foods.
2. Maintain ideal body weight.
3. Avoid too much fat, especially saturated fat and cholesterol.
4. Avoid too much sugar.
5. Avoid too much sodium.
6. Eat foods with adequate starch and fiber.
7. Drink alcohol in moderation, if at all.

Sound demanding? Not really.

The most difficult requirement for compliance is found between the lines; we need to learn to care enough about ourselves to want to improve our present nutritional status and that of our children.

The collection of recipes printed on the pages that follow generally comply with the tenets of the Guidelines. While not all recipes are in strict compliance, the majority of selections favor moderation in calories, saturated fat, sodium, and sugar. In addition, you can make an informed choice because each recipe is profiled for its approximate calorie, protein, fat, carbohydrate, and sodium content. Many of the recipes also have useful comments about their nutritional strengths and weaknesses, often with hints on how the end product can be strengthened.

In some cases, substitutions are offered as well. For example, plain yogurt is suggested where sour cream might traditionally be called for; milk is substituted for cream when feasible; light cream replaces the heavy variety in many instances; and skim milk ricotta cheese is offered as the preferable alternative to the whole-milk-based cheese. These changes reduce the saturated fat content.

Suggestions for using fresh, unprocessed foods are made whenever possible, thereby discouraging use of canned goods or processed meats or cheeses. In the spice and herb department, only the fresh or powdered forms rather than the "salts" are called for, as for example garlic powder is recommended over garlic salt.

This book attempts to combine a consciousness about health and an appreciation for good taste. And herein is the challenge before so many parents: to cultivate within their offspring a desire to eat not simply to satisfy hunger or derive pleasure from food, but also because food, chosen with care, is essential to feeling and looking good.

An understanding of what is the appropriate nutrition program for your child is only half the battle; the real challenge lies in execution— how to make the program work for your child.

Children will be motivated only if the reasons are meaningful to them, such as improved performance on the track team, or a better likelihood of making the cheerleader squad. The objective is to begin instilling the advantages and values of proper nutrition early in life, gradually and simply, without pressure.

There are obstacles, however, continually thwarting the development of sound eating habits and attitudes toward food; and these obstacles are broad in scope and influence. Consider the power of advertising. An effective television campaign can have us confusing our food needs with our food wants. Peer pressure is another potent obstacle. The very human need to be accepted exists among children and adults alike, which can make saying "no" to an offering rather difficult. And in today's fast-paced life, the temptation to choose convenience over nutrition is considerable.

While there are no simple solutions to creating just the right environment for cultivating sound eating habits among our children, here are several suggestions for making the world of food a more balanced, meaningful, and healthy place in which to eat.

■ A child responds best to child-size servings. It is far better to offer small servings and let the child ask for second helpings than to load the plate with an adult-size portion. Too big a serving can be intimidating, or, on the other hand, be the beginning of overeating.

■ Utensils that are easy to manipulate encourage self-feeding and independence. Spoons and forks with straight, short handles, a broad-mouthed cup, a dish with sides and divided compartments are examples.

■ Easy to clean, durable materials placed on the table for eating, and over the table for protection, decrease anxiety for all at mealtimes. Should something drop to the floor, there will be no breakage, and spills are easily cleaned up.

■ Color and texture are important factors in a child's acceptance or rejection of food. Bright colors attract a child—the orange of carrots, the bright green of early peas, and the natural color of strawberries, for example; crunchy foods like sweet, raw vegetables, whole wheat crackers, or fresh apple wedges are generally well accepted by kids, as are smooth and cool foods like puddings, custards, yogurt, and ice cream. Mixed textures, like a soggy cold cereal in milk, or a semi-soft vegetable (broccoli or cauliflower), can cause problems.

■ A relaxed, happy mealtime environment is essential to a healthy attitude toward food and eating. The dinner table is not the forum for arguments or discipline.

■ Mild, delicate flavors please a young palate, rather than spicy or complex flavors. Take advantage of a child's inherent accept-ance of food in its natural state. Salt, gravy, ketchup, sugar, and other condiments are unnecessary additives that become nec-essary as a result of learned behavior.

■ Desserts need not become "a forbidden fruit" if they are served nonchalantly as part of the meal. Wholesome choices like custard, fruits, whole grain or molasses cookies, and ice milk make a positive contribution to health and growth. Desserts can indeed supply the diet with nutrients that might otherwise not be consumed. Pies, cakes, and pastries generally have little redeeming nutritional value, but in moderation, they too can have a place in the diet.

■ Forcing a child to eat interrupts the development of sound food habits. A child is often the best judge of how much is enough. None of us is born with an automatic membership in the "clean plate club," and joining can be the source of a life-long problem of overeating.

■ Let the children get involved in food preparation and meal service. A feeling of usefulness may result in a healthy interest in eating, particularly among the picky eaters. Have them set the table, or perhaps make the salad, or prepare the meat loaf. En-courage self-service as well.

■ Finger foods make eating less of a challenge for the small folk. Sandwich quarters, raw vegetable nibbles, and fruits, cheese, or meats cut into bite-size pieces, are more likely to be accepted than if presented in adult style.

It is important that a variety of nutritious and appealing foods be served in appropriate and appealing ways, by parents who main-tain a relaxed attitude about what, how much, and particularly why their child eats. This not only builds healthy food habits, but encourages consumption of a variety of essential nutrients, and can actually foster a child's sense of trust in the outside world.

Indeed, food is more than just something to eat.

—Alexis M. Beck

1 thick slice protein or whole grain bread
1 tablespoon margarine, or more depending on size of skillet

1 egg
Salt and pepper to taste

Cut a hole in the middle of the piece of bread, large enough to contain the egg. Melt margarine in skillet and brown bread on one side. Flip, and carefully crack egg, dropping it into the hole so as not to break the yolk. Cover skillet and simmer slowly until egg firms.

Serves 1

Per serving:
Calories: 255
Sodium: 1,530 mg.

Protein: 9 g.
Fat: 16 g.
Carbohydrate: 15 g.

EGGNOG

1 glass milk
1 egg

1½ teaspoons honey
½ teaspoon vanilla

Stir in blender.

This is the easiest way to get an egg down on a hurried morning.

Serves 1

Nutrition Note: The benefits include high-quality protein, vitamin A, and iron. As a breakfast drink, it provides the foundation for a healthy day and good food habits.

Per serving:
Calories: 277
Sodium: 185 mg.

Protein: 15 g.
Fat: 15 g.
Carbohydrate: 20 g.

1 tablespoon margarine	½ teaspoon salt
3 eggs, separated	⅛ teaspoon pepper
½ cup cottage cheese	1 teaspoon chives
3 tablespoons milk	

Preheat oven to 350°F. Melt margarine in 10-inch skillet. Beat egg whites until stiff. Place yolks, cottage cheese, milk, salt, pepper, and chives in blender and run on high speed for 1 minute. Pour over egg whites and fold in gently. Slide into hot skillet, cooking ½ minute on high and lower to simmer until bottom is firm and lightly browned. Place skillet in oven and bake 10 minutes or until lightly browned on top. Fold and serve immediately.

Serves 4

Nutrition Note: Protein and calcium all folded up in a light, tasty omelette that might tempt even the most ardent egg refuser.

Per serving:	Protein: 10 g.
Calories: 143	Fat: 9 g.
Sodium: 445 mg.	Carbohydrate: 2 g.

EASY CHEESE SOUFFLE

3 eggs, separated	¼ teaspoon salt
¼ pound Cheddar cheese	Dash cayenne pepper
¼ cup evaporated milk	

Preheat oven to 325°F. Beat egg whites until stiff. Melt the cheese in the top of a double boiler, adding milk gradually and stirring until sauce is smooth. Add seasonings and slowly mix in egg yolks. Cool. Fold the beaten egg white into the mix and pour into a small greased casserole. Bake for 20 minutes, or until firm.

Serves 4

Nutrition Note: If getting your child to drink milk is a problem, here's a dish that will supplement the daily calcium requirement.

Per serving:	Protein: 27 g.
Calories: 355	Fat: 26 g.
Sodium: 795 mg.	Carbohydrate: 3 g.

BUCKWHEAT PANCAKES

1 cup buckwheat flour	2 teaspoons baking powder
1 cup whole wheat flour	2 cups milk
½ teaspoon salt	2 eggs, beaten
1 tablespoon brown sugar	1 tablespoon cooking oil

Sift buckwheat flour, which tends to be lumpy, and stir in other dry ingredients. Add milk, eggs, and oil. Cook on hot, lightly oiled griddle. (If pancakes are too thick for your taste, add more milk.)

Makes 18

Per serving (3):   Protein: 10 g.
Calories: 234   Fat: 8 g.
Sodium: 364 mg.   Carbohydrate: 32 g.

OLD-FASHIONED PANCAKES

½ cup wheat germ	1 teaspoon salt
2 cups whole wheat flour	2 eggs
2 teaspoons baking powder	2½–3 cups milk
1 tablespoon brown sugar	2 tablespoons oil

Mix dry ingredients first and then add the liquids, stirring thoroughly. For thinner pancakes, add more milk. Cook on hot, ungreased griddle.

For variety, add one of the following:
1 cup cooked corn, drained if from a can
1 apple, peeled, cored, and diced
fresh blueberries, raspberries, or strawberries

Serve with maple syrup; or try spreading with applesauce for a change.

Makes 18

Nutrition Note: A whole grain variety of this traditional favorite—supplying the diet with vitamins B_2, B_3, B_6, and E.

Per serving (3):   Protein: 17 g.
Calories: 355   Fat: 12 g.
Sodium: 325 mg.   Carbohydrate: 45 g.

1 cup soy nuts	¼ cup vegetable oil
1 cup sesame seeds	¼ cup honey
1 cup sunflower seeds	1 cup rye or wheat flakes
3 cups wheat germ	2 tablespoons Torula yeast
2 cups rolled oats	½ cup dried apricots or
1 cup bran	prunes, chopped
½ cup soy flour	1 cup raisins

Preheat oven to 350 °F. Toast nuts and seeds, stirring frequently. Then chop them in a grinder (or blender if you do not have a grinder, but just ¼ cup at a time and only for a few seconds), and set aside. Mix the rest of the ingredients except for dried fruit and raisins and place on a cookie sheet with sides, or in a roasting pan. Toast in oven for 45 minutes, stirring frequently. Add seeds, nuts, and fruit and store in refrigerator in plastic bag with a wire tie.

One serving of granola with milk in the morning will keep up the old energy all morning long!

Makes approximately 11 cups

Nutrition Note: While not low in calories, this crunchy granola is high in iron, B vitamins, fiber, and fun; wonderful as a morning cereal or a nutritious afternoon snack.

Per serving (½ cup):   Protein: 14 g.
Calories: 320   Fat: 14 g.
Sodium: 6 mg.   Carbohydrate: 35 g.

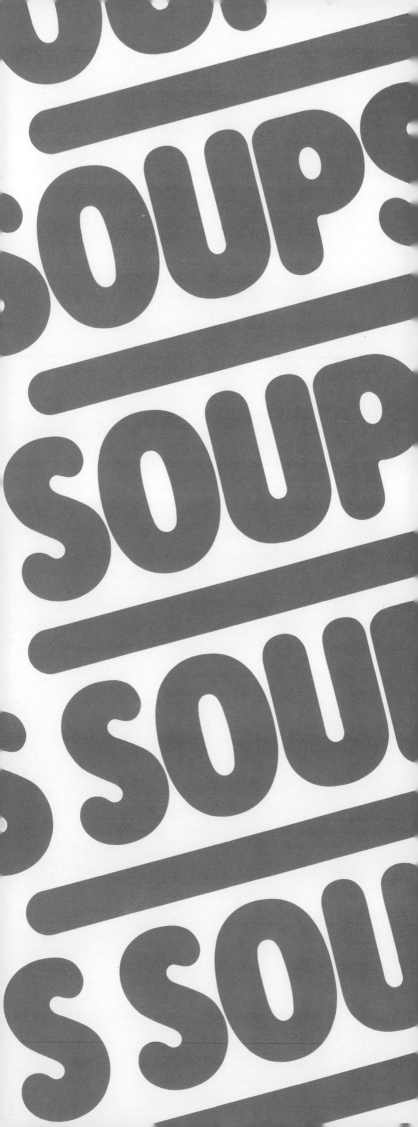

½ cup flour
1 chicken, skinned and cut in small pieces
½ stick margarine
1 onion, chopped
1 clove garlic, chopped
1 large can tomatoes, chopped coarsely

4 bay leaves
1 teaspoon salt
¼ teaspoon cayenne pepper
1 tablespoon parsley
2 cups okra
1 cup seafood (oysters, scallops, shrimp, or crab)
2 tablespoons gumbo filé*

Place flour in paper bag and drop in chicken; shake well and brown chicken in skillet with melted margarine. Place browned chicken in soup pot with onion, garlic, tomatoes, bay leaves, salt, pepper, and parsley. Cover with water and simmer for an hour. Then add okra and seafood and simmer an additional 5–10 minutes. Add gumbo filé at the very last moment for a 1-minute simmer.

*Gumbo filé can be purchased in specialty shops. One bottle goes a long way and is well worth keeping in your stock!

Serves 6

Per serving:
Calories: 334
Sodium: 782 mg.

Protein: 23 g.
Fat: 17 g.
Carbohydrate: 22 g.

1 tablespoon margarine	6 cups water
¼ cup vegetable oil	2 teaspoons salt
1½ cups chopped onion	⅓ cup uncooked brown rice
4 cups chopped carrots	3 teaspoons honey
3 ounces tomato paste	2½ cups milk
1 cup chopped apples	1 cup raisins (optional)

Melt margarine and oil in a soup pot and sauté onions and carrots until the onions are transparent. Stir in tomato paste, apples, stock, and salt. Bring to a boil and stir in the rice. Cover and simmer about 30–45 minutes or until the soup is pretty orange and the carrots are tender. Puree in blender. When ready to serve, add milk and reheat. To use the raisins, add them to the milk, and heat until they are plump.

Serves 6

Nutrition Note: Loaded with vitamins, iron, calcium, protein, and flavor. Serve this soup with a grilled cheese sandwich on a brisk winter's day.

Per serving:	Protein: 8 g.
Calories: 388	Fat: 15 g.
Sodium: 1,012 mg.	Carbohydrate: 55 g.

CORN CHOWDER

4 large potatoes	1 tablespoon margarine
2 large onions	1 quart milk
1 can creamed corn	Salt and pepper

Peel and cube potatoes and mince onions. Place in saucepan with small amount of water and simmer until tender and water is almost evaporated. Add the corn, margarine, and milk, and simmer, stirring, for 5 minutes. Season with salt and pepper to taste.

Serves 4–6

Nutrition Note: Usually popular among children, this version of corn chowder is particularly rich in calcium, protein, and homemade flavor.

Per serving:	Protein: 9 g.
Calories: 279	Fat: 8 g.
Sodium: 415 mg.	Carbohydrate: 42 g.

FIREMAN'S SOUP

1 pound soup beef, cut in
   1-inch cubes
1 soup bone
2 large carrots,
   peeled and sliced
1 large turnip,
   peeled and sliced

4 stalks celery, including
   leaves, thickly sliced
2 potatoes, peeled and sliced
1 large can tomatoes
2 bay leaves
¼ cup chopped parsley
Salt and pepper to taste

Place 2 quarts of water in a large pot and add all ingredients. Simmer slowly for 45 minutes, tasting occasionally for seasoning. If you like a thick soup, you can add ⅛ cup uncooked rice at beginning of cooking time, but the kids whose favorite this is like to pick out the vegetables from a clear soup.

This is a surprising favorite with babies just learning to eat with their own hands—if served to them, the meat should first be cut into tiny bits.

Serves 6

Per serving:
Calories: 287
Sodium: 470 mg.

Protein: 17 g.
Fat: 15 g.
Carbohydrate: 20 g.

FRUIT SOUP

3 cups fruit juice
   (unsweetened orange,
   apple, or pineapple)
1 banana
1 apple, peeled and chopped
1 peach, peeled and chopped
½ to 1 cup sliced
   strawberries
⅛ cantaloupe, cut into
   bite-size pieces

1 tablespoon fresh lemon
   juice
½ teaspoon fresh mint,
   chopped
½ teaspoon cinnamon
¼ teaspoon nutmeg
1 tablespoon honey (optional)
1 cup plain yogurt or
   buttermilk

Combine all ingredients in a blender and whirl to desired consistency. Serve in tall mugs topped with a dollop of yogurt and a fresh strawberry or a sprig of mint.

Makes 6 servings

Nutrition Note: Try your own variations on this wonderfully light, satisfying, and vitamin-packed "soup," using seasonal fruits. Serve for breakfast, lunch, dessert, or an afternoon snack.

Per serving:
Calories: 148
Sodium: 21 mg.

Protein: 1 g.
Fat: 1 g.
Carbohydrate: 34 g.

¾ cup split peas
1 onion
2 carrots, peeled
1 large bay leaf
6 cups water
2 teaspoons salt

⅛ teaspoon pepper
¼ teaspoon basil
¼ cup parsley, chopped
3 cups zucchini, diced
  (optional)
1 pound spinach (optional)

Simmer split peas, onion, carrots, and bay leaf in 4 cups of the water for 30 minutes. If you are using zucchini, add it 10 minutes before this time is up. Then remove the bay leaf and puree stock in blender. Pour through sieve back into the soup pot and add additional 2 cups of water. Add the salt, pepper, basil, and parsley, and if you are using spinach, add it now. Cook several minutes, adjusting seasoning.

It is very important to sieve this stock thoroughly. Kids shudder at the lumps in pea soup, not the taste!

Serves 6

Nutrition Note: Served with a slice of crusty whole grain bread, a glass of milk, and a cup of fresh fruit salad, our Pea Soup becomes the center of a nutritious, convenient, and hearty meal with wide appeal.

Per serving:
Calories: 108
Sodium: 791 mg.

Protein: 69 g.
Fat: trace
Carbohydrate: 20 g.

Right: Apple Nut Salad, recipe page 34

½ cup cooked brown rice
2 cups cleaned shrimp
¼ medium onion, diced
1 stalk celery, diced
6 sprigs parsley, chopped

½ green pepper, diced
2 cups canned tomatoes
1 teaspoon salt
1 teaspoon chili powder

Place all ingredients in large saucepan and simmer slowly for 10 minutes.

Serves 4

Per serving:
Calories: 150
Sodium: 759 mg.

Protein: 20 g.
Fat: 1 g.
Carbohydrate: 14 g.

TUNA PEA CASSEROLE 25

1 package dry chicken noodle
  soup mix
2½ cups water
3 tablespoons margarine
3 tablespoons flour

½ teaspoon salt
⅛ teaspoon pepper
7-ounce can tuna, drained
1 cup peas, fresh or frozen
Bread crumbs

Preheat oven to 350°F. Cook soup mix in boiling water. Meanwhile, melt margarine and add flour and seasonings slowly to thicken. Add this to the soup and simmer 5 minutes. Combine with tuna and peas in a 1-quart casserole dish. Cover with bread crumbs and bake 15 minutes.

Note: Another way to make this dish is to substitute a can of mushroom soup for the chicken noodle and add 2 cups of cooked noodles.

Serves 4

Per serving:
Calories: 273
Sodium: 1,460 mg.

Protein: 17 g.
Fat: 6 g.
Carbohydrate: 20 g.

1 ½ pounds ground beef
1 large onion, diced
Salt and pepper
½ cup celery, diced
6 slices of mild cheese

2 cups tomatoes
1 cup water
2 cups macaroni
½ cup green olives (optional)

In a large skillet, sauté ground beef and onion until browned, seasoning to taste. Add the remaining ingredients and simmer, covered, 30 minutes or until macaroni is done.

Serves 4

Per serving:
Calories: 700
Sodium: 862 mg.

Protein: 56 g.
Fat: 30 g.
Carbohydrate: 51 g.

PIZZA BURGERS

1 onion, diced
1 pound ground beef
4 ounces chili sauce
1 teaspoon oregano

½ teaspoon parsley flakes
1 teaspoon thyme
Grated cheese
6 hamburger buns, sliced

Sauté onion and ground beef in skillet until browned. Add chili sauce, oregano, parsley flakes, and thyme, and simmer slowly until thick enough to spread. Spread mixture on buns and top with grated cheese. Pop under the broiler until the cheese melts.

12 pieces

Nutrition Note: You might try experimenting with a whole wheat (or enriched) version of the "all-American hamburger bun."

Per serving (2):
Calories: 31.1
Sodium: 190 mg.

Protein: 21 g.
Fat: 10 g.
Carbohydrate: 34 g.

1 box taco shells
1 ½ pounds lean ground beef
1 large onion, chopped
2 teaspoons chili powder
¾ teaspoon oregano
¾ teaspooon paprika
½ teaspoon ground cumin
½ teaspoon pepper
1 ½ teaspoons
   Worcestershire sauce
1 cup tomato sauce

Garlic powder to taste
1 small head lettuce, shredded
1 tomato, thinly wedged
1 avocado, peeled, seeded,
   sliced
1 cup plain yogurt
¼ cup plain olives, sliced
   (optional)
½ cup grated cheese
   (Monterey Jack or
   Cheddar)

Warm taco shells in 350°F oven for 10 minutes. Meanwhile, brown ground beef in a large skillet over medium heat; drain fat. Add onion and sauté until limp. Stir in chili powder, oregano, paprika, cumin, pepper, Worcestershire, and tomato sauce. Simmer uncovered, stirring until hot. Season with garlic powder. Place remaining ingredients in separate dishes on the table. The kids fill the shells themselves, beginning with lettuce, then meat, and garnishing, as they choose, with tomato, avocado, yogurt, olives, and cheese.

Makes 10

Nutrition Note: Each taco is a balanced meal in itself, providing lots of protein, vitamins A and C, and calcium, not to mention a lot of fun!

Try serving with a glass of Fruit Sangria, reminiscent of the authentic Mexican beverage: Combine equal parts your choice of mixed fruit juices and club soda, garnished with fresh orange slices.

Per serving:
Calories: 318
Sodium: 306 mg.

Protein: 20 g.
Fat: 17 g.
Carbohydrate: 22 g.

3 cups dry beans, kidney
   or navy
½ medium onion, chopped
¾ cup water
1 apple, peeled and sliced
1 carrot, peeled and sliced

1 teaspoon dry mustard
½ cup Ketchup
   (see p. 124)
1 pound ground beef
   or ½ pound all-beef
   frankfurters (optional)

Preheat oven to 350°F. Cook beans according to package directions. Sauté onion in a small amount of oil and drain, wiping out skillet with paper towel. Return onions to skillet, and add water, apples, and carrots and simmer, covered, for 5 minutes. Mash. Add remaining ingredients and stir. If you use franks, cut them in bite-size chunks and stir in now. If you use ground beef, sauté separately and add now. Bake, covered, for 45 minutes.

Serves 8

Nutrition Note: Combined with a whole grain bread, baked beans provide all the protein a healthy person needs at a meal...without the expense of meat. Lots of iron and fiber in this recipe.

For a real treat, and a taste of old tradition, serve Country-Style Baked Beans with Boston Brown Bread (see page 73) and re-create the "Saturday Night Supper" New Englanders have been enjoying for 200 years.

Per serving:
Calories: 140
Sodium: 190 mg.

Protein: 8 g.
Fat: 0.5 g.
Carbohydrate: 26 g.

Right: Calico Beans, recipe page 31

½ pound bacon
4 stalks celery, diced
1 green pepper, diced
1 large onion, minced

1 cup rice, cooked according to directions (about 4 cups cooked)
½ teaspoon basil
¼ teaspoon pepper
2-pound can tomatoes

Preheat oven to 350°F. Sauté bacon until crisp, remove from skillet, and drain. In the same skillet, sauté celery, green pepper, and onion until softened. Combine these ingredients with cooked rice in a casserole dish. Add remaining ingredients, cutting in tomatoes, and stir. If necessary, add a small amount of water as the rice absorbs liquid. Bake 1 hour.

This is a tasty and inexpensive dish, good for a sit-down party of children.

Serves 6–8

Nutrition Note: Suggest using nitrite-free bacon now available in the supermarket... while it may not last as long in the refrigerator, it's free of the controversial preservative sodium nitrite.

Per serving:
Calories: 390
Sodium: 305 mg.

Protein: 8 g.
Fat: 25 g.
Carbohydrate: 33 g.

HAM AND SPINACH SOUFFLÉ

1 pound spinach, washed and cooked until wilted
½ cup milk
3 eggs, separated
¼ onion

¼ teaspoon salt
⅛ teaspoon pepper
2 slices stale whole grain or protein bread
1 cup cooked ham, cubed

Preheat oven to 350°F. Place approximately half of the spinach in a blender with milk and egg yolks, and puree. Slowly add onion, seasonings, and bread pieces, pushing ingredients toward blade with rubber spatula. Add remaining spinach. Beat egg whites with electric beater until stiff and peaky. Fold the spinach mixture and ham into the egg whites. Pour into a 1-quart greased casserole and bake 45–50 minutes until firm.

A delicious budget stretcher!

Serves 4

Per serving:
Calories: 198
Sodium: 267 mg.

Protein: 19 g.
Fat: 9 g.
Carbohydrate: 10 g.

Right: Shrimp Jambalaya, recipe page 24

Whole Wheat Pie Crust
(see p. 125),
enough for 1 large or
2 small pies.
1 onion, diced

3 dashes cayenne pepper
½ teaspoon dried mustard
3 eggs
1½ cups milk
1 ounce melted margarine

Preheat oven to 350°F. Rip Swiss cheese in pieces and cover base of crusts with it. Spread onto this the diced onion. Blend eggs, milk, melted margarine, salt, pepper, and mustard in blender. Pour into pie. Bake 30 minutes or until crust is nicely browned and center is firm.

Serves 6

Per serving:
Calories: 555
Sodium: 1,122 mg.

Protein: 21 g.
Fat: 37 g.
Carbohydrate: 34 g.

Right: Fruit Soup, recipe page 20

THE VEGGIE

4 large fresh mushrooms
2 green peppers
2 medium tomatoes
1 medium zucchini

4 slices whole grain or
pumpernickel bread
4 slices mozzarella or
Muenster cheese

Preheat oven to 350°F. Remove stems from mushrooms. Chop green pepper, tomatoes, and zucchini into bite-size pieces, and toss together. Pile vegetable mixture on bread slices, forming a small hill. Top with mushroom caps. Cover completely with cheese. Bake 10 to 15 minutes or until cheese melts.

Serves 4

Nutrition Note: The Veggie may win your kids' award for the most nutritious while delicious sandwich they have ever tried. It's fun for them to make, too! Wonderful for Saturday lunch or a light supper.

Per serving:
Calories: 307
Sodium: 410 mg.

Protein: 20 g.
Fat: 16 g.
Carbohydrate: 20 g.

Assorted vegetables, such as carrots, potatoes, peas, zucchini, beans, and/or any of your children's favorites, in appropriate quantities for your meal and cut in bite-size chunks

Sliced onion
Salt to taste
Bovril or beef bouillon to taste
Garlic powder to taste
Chopped parsley
All-beef frankfurters, cut in 1-inch chunks

Bring 2 quarts of water to a boil in a large pot. Add all ingredients except frankfurters and simmer about 30 minutes. Add frankfurter bits 10 minutes before soup is done.

Leftovers can be frozen and served another time.

CALICO BEANS

15½-ounce can kidney beans
15-ounce can lima beans
1-pound can pork and beans
½ cup Ketchup (see p. 124)

1 onion, minced
1 tablespoon prepared mustard
2 tablespoons vinegar
2 tablespoons honey

Preheat oven to 350°F. Place all the ingredients in a casserole, stir, and bake 30–45 minutes.

Serves 4–6

Per serving:
Calories: 321
Sodium: 576 mg.

Protein: 14 g.
Fat: 4 g.
Carbohydrate: 56 g.

34   APPLE NUT SALAD

½ cup mayonnaise
1 tablespoon lemon juice
Salt and pepper to taste
2 cups diced apples

1 cup diced celery
½ cup chopped walnuts
½ cup raisins

Combine mayonnaise, lemon juice, and seasonings for a dressing. Toss with combination of apples, celery, nuts, and raisins, and serve.

Serves 4

Per serving:
Calories: 408
Sodium: 347 mg.

Protein: 2 g.
Fat: 31 g.
Carbohydrate: 30 g.

Right: Eggnog, recipe page 12

RAW CARROT SALAD

1 bunch of carrots,
  peeled and grated
1 small onion, grated
⅔ tablespoon vinegar

⅔ tablespoon sugar
1 cup mayonnaise
Salt, pepper, and celery salt
  to taste

Grate the vegetables first, and then mix the dressing. Toss.

Note: This is also delicious and attractive with raisins or fresh pineapple chunks.

Serves 4

Nutrition Note: Full of flavor, crunch, and vitamin A, potassium, and fiber, too!

Per serving:
Calories: 425
Sodium: 625 mg.

Protein: 1 g.
Fat: 29 g.
Carbohydrate: 40 g.

CRUNCHY ORANGE SALAD

1 envelope unflavored gelatin
1 cup orange juice
1 cup shredded carrots
1 cup raisins

½ 8-ounce can crushed
  pineapple
1 tablespoon honey

Dissolve the gelatin in the orange juice by heating slowly in a small saucepan. Remove and add the rest of the ingredients. Chill in refrigerator until set.

This can be served plain or with a topping of creamed cottage cheese.

Serves 6

Nutrition Note: Nutritious, delicious, and guaranteed to please a crowd of young people.

Per serving:
Calories: 129
Sodium: 7 mg.

Protein: 2 g.
Fat: 0 g.
Carbohydrate: 30 g.

CRANBERRY NUT SALAD

1 envelope unflavored gelatin
1 cup hot water
½ cup cold water
½ cup crushed pineapple,
  drained

¼ cup walnuts, chopped
1 small orange or tangerine,
  sectioned
1-pound can whole-cranberry
  sauce

Mix gelatin with hot water until dissolved. Add cold water and chill until partially thickened. Stir in the rest of the ingredients evenly and chill thoroughly.

Serves 6

Nutrition Note: Smooth, cool, and a not-too-sweet source of vitamin C.

Per serving:
Calories: 93
Sodium: 1 mg.

Protein: 1 g.
Fat: 3 g.
Carbohydrate: 16 g.

FRESH SPINACH AND TANGERINE SALAD

1 pound fresh spinach
3 tangerines, peeled and
  sectioned, or 1 can
  mandarin oranges

Vinaigrette Dressing
(see p. 128)

Thoroughly wash spinach and break into small pieces, removing stems. Add tangerines and dressing and serve.

Note: If your child likes raw sliced mushrooms, they can be substituted for the tangerines.

Serves 6

Per serving:			Vinaigrette Dressing
Calories:	31	+	165
Sodium:	60 mg.	+	415 mg.
Protein:	3 g.	+	0 g.
Fat:	0 g.	+	18 g.
Carbohydrate:	5 g.	+	1 g.

COLESLAW WITH...

½ head of large cabbage
2 carrots
½ cup raisins

½ cup mayonnaise
¼ cup lemon juice or vinegar
Salt and pepper

Shred cabbage and carrots. Combine with raisins. Mix mayonnaise, lemon juice, salt, and pepper to taste. Toss together.

Cabbage is a fine source of vitamin C and is available, cheap, all year round. Some children prefer its milder taste to salad greens with a sharper dressing.

Note: Instead of carrots you can substitute diced apples or pineapple chunks.

Serves 4

Per serving:
Calories: 263
Sodium: 130 mg.

Protein: 1 g.
Fat: 14 g.
Carbohydrate: 32 g.

4 cups chunked cooked
  chicken
2 cups celery, thinly sliced

1 cup walnuts, chopped
1 large can peach slices
  or 1 cup fresh peaches

Dressing:

¼ cup juice of peaches
¼ cup mayonnaise

1 cup heavy cream, whipped

Toss dressing with salad ingredients just before serving. Place on crisp lettuce leaves.

Serves 4–6

Per serving:
Calories: 511
Sodium: 155 mg.

Protein: 35 g.
Fat: 35 g.
Carbohydrate: 13 g.

MARINER'S MACARONI

8-ounce package elbow
  macaroni
1 large can tuna
2 tablespoons diced onion
¼ cup sliced radishes
  (optional)
¼ cup diced green pepper

¾ cup mayonnaise
1 teaspoon salt
¼ teaspoon dried basil leaves
3 tablespoons lemon juice
  or vinegar
2 medium tomatoes
1 cucumber

Boil macaroni and drain. Drain tuna, mash, and add to cooked macaroni. Add onion, radish, and pepper. Mix mayonnaise with salt, basil, and lemon juice. Toss in the salad and garnish with tomato and cucumber slices.

Serves 6

Per serving:
Calories: 325
Sodium: 715 mg.

Protein: 17 g.
Fat: 27 g.
Carbohydrate: 5 g.

1¼ pounds fresh or
  2 packages frozen chopped
  broccoli
2 tablespoons mayonnaise

2 tablespoons yogurt
Juice of 1 fresh lemon
½ cup sliced stuffed green
  olives

Preheat oven to 350°F. Thaw frozen broccoli in saucepan as directed on package, but do not cook. Drain any excess liquid (most should have evaporated while heating). Add rest of ingredients and mix. Bake in greased casserole dish about 30 minutes.

Serves 6

Nutrition Note: If you want to keep the sodium content down, keep the olive count down.

Per serving:
Calories: 68
Sodium: 120 mg.

Protein: 3 g.
Fat: 4 g.
Carbohydrate: 5 g.

CARROT NESTS

One attractive way to serve carrots is to shred them, then steam in a small amount of salted water until they are done (and water has evaporated). Then make nests on the plate. You can add a teaspoon of honey to sweeten, and serve with a dab of margarine or butter.

Nutrition Note: As a garnish or a side dish, to add interest as well as nutrition to the meal.

Per serving (½ cup):
Calories: 35
Sodium: 60 mg.

Protein: 1 g.
Fat: 5 g.
Carbohydrate: 21 g.

1 package frozen chopped broccoli
1 package frozen chopped spinach
11-ounce can cream of mushroom soup

2 tomatoes, sliced
1 onion, sliced in rings
½ cup bread crumbs
¼ cup melted margarine

Preheat oven to 325°F. Cook vegetables slightly, until just thawed. Combine with undiluted mushroom soup and pour into a low baking dish. Top with tomato and onion rings. Sprinkle bread crumbs on top, and pour on melted margarine. Bake 35 minutes.

Serves 6

Nutrition Note: A great way to present some of those often-neglected, vitamin-rich vegetables.

Per serving:
Calories: 164
Sodium: 525 mg.

Protein: 2 g.
Fat: 11 g.
Carbohydrate: 13 g.

GLAZED CARROTS

12 small carrots, peeled
4 tablespoons margarine
1 tablespoon brown sugar
2 tablespoons honey

¼ teaspoon grated orange rind
1 tablespoon orange juice
2–3 tablespoons chopped parsley

Simmer carrots whole in salted water until tender. Blend remaining ingredients, except for parsley, in another saucepan. Add the tender carrots and sauté them slowly until glazed. Roll in chopped parsley.

Serves 6

Nutrition Note: A zesty package of vitamin A and a taste of the islands....

Per serving:
Calories: 161
Sodium: 122 mg.

Protein: 2 g.
Fat: 7 g.
Carbohydrate: 21 g.

42   EGGPLANT CASSEROLE

1 medium-size eggplant	Salt and pepper to taste
2 peppers, green or red	Bread crumbs
2 medium onions	2 tablespoons margarine
2 eggs	
8-ounce can tomato sauce	
or 3 fresh tomatoes, sliced	

Preheat oven to 375°F. Peel and slice the eggplant. Cut peppers and onions into rings. Beat the eggs in a small amount of water. If you are using tomato sauce, add egg mix to it now. Layer vegetables, including fresh tomatoes if you are using them, in a greased casserole dish. Pour egg mix over vegetables, adding seasonings and water so that liquid half covers the vegetables. Top with bread crumbs and dot with margarine. Bake 1 hour.

Note: Other vegetables can also be added to this dish, such as peas, summer squash, beans, or zucchini.

Serves 4–6

Nutrition Note: Just a hint of Italy, right in your own kitchen...and watch the results disappear. A wonderful way to supplement the family's diet with vitamins A, C, B_6, and potassium.

Per serving:	Protein: 5 g.
Calories: 120	Fat: 3 g.
Sodium: 530 mg.	Carbohydrate: 19 g.

CARROT SOUFFLÉ

4 fresh carrots	½ teaspoon salt
3 tablespoons margarine	⅛ teaspoon pepper
3 tablespoons flour	4 eggs, separated
1 cup milk	

Peel and slice carrots. Boil gently, in just enough water to cover, until tender. Drain and mash. Force through a sieve or whirl in blender for a minute or two. Melt margarine in a skillet. Blend in flour. Gradually add milk and cook, stirring until smooth and thickened. Add salt and pepper. Beat egg whites until stiff but not dry. Set aside. Beat egg yolks until light and lemon-colored, and add them to cooled mixture. Add carrot pulp and mix. Fold half of egg whites into carrot mixture, then fold in remaining half. Grease a 2-quart soufflé or casserole dish and fill with carrot mixture. Bake at 375°F for 30 minutes or until puffy and lightly browned on top.

Serves 4

Nutrition Note: Very light, yet satisfying. A particularly rich source of vitamin A that would complement an assortment of foods...from fish to fowl to flank steak.

Per serving:	Protein: 10 g.
Calories: 240	Fat: 17 g.
Sodium: 800 mg.	Carbohydrate: 12 g.

2 acorn squash
2 apples
1 ½ teaspoons grated lemon
  peel
1 tablespoon fresh lemon
  juice

2 tablespoons margarine,
  melted
⅓ cup firmly packed brown
  sugar
¼ teaspoon salt
Cinnamon

Cut squash into halves lengthwise and scoop out seedy centers. Place cut side down in baking dish and pour in boiling water to a ½-inch depth. Bake in a 400°F oven 25 minutes. While squash bakes, pare, core, and dice apples. Mix with lemon peel and juice, margarine, and sugar. Sprinkle squash halves with salt and cinnamon and fill with apple mixture. Cover and bake 30 minutes more (replace water if evaporated).

Serves 4

Per serving:
Calories: 258
Sodium: 225 mg.

Protein: 3 g.
Fat: 6 g.
Carbohydrate: 48 g.

CORNFLAKES AND CAULIFLOWER

1 medium head cauliflower
1 stick of melted margarine

1 cup crushed cornflakes
1 teaspoon Aromat (optional)

Steam cauliflower whole over boiling, salted water, until tender enough to eat. Drop the cornflakes into the melted margarine until the mix achieves a damp but still crispy consistency. Cap the cauliflower with the crumb crust and serve. If you can find a bottle of Aromat, a few shakes of this Swedish spice will add to the flavor.

Serves 4–6

Nutrition Note: So simple to prepare, yet adds a gourmet flair and some worthwhile vitamin C!

Per serving:
Calories: 170
Sodium: 37 mg.

Protein: 3 g.
Fat: 15 g.
Carbohydrate: 7 g.

CREAMED SPINACH AND MUSHROOMS

½ pound fresh mushrooms
4 tablespoons margarine
2 pounds fresh spinach
1 cup light cream

½ teaspoon salt
⅛ teaspoon pepper
3 tablespoons flour

Sauté mushrooms in 2 tablespoons of margarine. Wash the spinach and cook in the water that clings to its leaves until it wilts. Melt the remaining margarine in a skillet, add cream, seasonings, and flour to thicken. Place spinach and cream sauce in a blender and run on low speed until spinach goes through the blades once. Add mushrooms and serve.

Serves 6

Nutrition Note: Thought they wouldn't eat their spinach? Well, try this, with all its benefits of vitamins A and C and some of that hard-to-find iron.

Per serving:
Calories: 225
Sodium: 425 mg.

Protein: 8 g.
Fat: 16 g.
Carbohydrate: 15 g.

SUMMER SQUASH CASSEROLE

1 stick margarine
1 8-ounce package herb
    stuffing
2 summer squash
1 onion, sliced
3 medium carrots, peeled
    and sliced

1 jar pimientos
1 cup mushrooms, sliced
1 can cream of chicken soup
1 8-ounce container of plain
    yogurt
Salt, pepper, and celery salt
    to taste

Preheat oven to 350°F. Melt the margarine and pour half the stuffing into it, stirring until bread is moistened. Mix remaining ingredients in a large bowl. Spoon a layer of stuffing on the bottom of a greased casserole dish. Cover with vegetable mixture. Top with dry stuffing. Cover the casserole and bake 30 minutes.

This will seduce the squash haters and the rest of the family with them.

Serves 4–6

Per serving:
Calories: 278
Sodium: 1,014 mg.

Protein: 6 g.
Fat: 19 g.
Carbohydrate: 24 g.

Whole Wheat Crumb Crust
  for a 9-inch pie (see p. 125)

Filling:

5 cups cooked and mashed butternut squash	¼ teaspoon salt
¼ cup softened margarine	¼ teaspoon nutmeg
¼ cup raisins	¼ teaspoon vanilla extract
	Honey to taste

Preheat oven to 350°F. Mix filling ingredients thoroughly and pour into the pie shell. Dust with cinnamon and bake for 50 minutes or until firm.

Some committed vegetable haters change their minds when presented with a vegetable pie!

Serves 6

Nutrition Note: Imagine a pie that's not only nutritious (rich in vitamin A and iron) and delicious, but moderate in calories as well.

Per serving: Protein: 3 g.
Calories: 242   Fat: 6 g.
Sodium: 195 mg.   Carbohydrate: 44 g.

BAKED TOMATO WITH SQUASH

½ cup wheat germ	2 tablespoons oil
4 large tomatoes	¼ cup Cheddar cheese
½ cup chopped summer squash	¼ teaspoon salt
1 large celery stalk, diced	¼ cup bread crumbs (approximately)
½ green pepper, diced	

Preheat oven to 350°F. Grease a small cookie sheet and sprinkle it with wheat germ. Slice tomatoes in thick pieces and place on sheet. Sauté onion, squash, celery, and pepper in oil. When hot, add cheese, salt, and enough bread crumbs to hold the mixture together. Spoon on top of tomatoes and sprinkle again with wheat germ. Bake 15–20 minutes.

Serves 6

Per serving: Protein: 7 g.
Calories: 157   Fat: 8 g.
Sodium: 180 mg.   Carbohydrate: 15 g.

PARSNIP BAKE

1 pound parsnips	⅛ teaspoon nutmeg
2 apples	¼ cup chopped walnuts (optional)
1 cup unsweetened apple juice	
2 tablespoons brown sugar	

Remove parsnip tops and peel. Cut in half lengthwise and remove woody centers. Place in saucepan in just enough water to cover. Boil until tender, approximately 10 minutes. Peel, core, and dice apples, and set aside. Blend apple juice with sugar and nutmeg. Drain parsnips and place in oven-proof dish, topping with apples. Pour apple juice mixture over. Bake at 350°F for 15 minutes. Sprinkle with nuts. Return to oven for an additional 5 to 10 minutes or until apples are tender.

Serves 6

Nutrition Note: Parsnips are an interesting source of potassium. Try them prepared this way.

Per serving: Protein: 2 g.
Calories: 152   Fat: 4 g.
Sodium: 14 mg.   Carbohydrate: 27 g.

CRUNCHY GREEN BEANS

2 cups cut green beans,
  fresh or frozen
2 tablespoons margarine
1 teaspoon grated onion
1 teaspoon lime juice

¾ cup cereal flakes,
  coarsely crumbled*
2 tablespoons parsley,
  chopped

Boil green beans until cooked, drain and keep warm. Sauté onions in margarine until margarine begins to brown. Add lime juice and cereal flakes. Mix to evenly coat. Toss into green beans and mix in parsley.

Serves 6

*Choose a vitamin-fortified corn or wheat flake-based breakfast cereal.

Nutrition Note: The benefits of this recipe include easy preparation, a delightfully surprising texture, and vitamins A, C, and members of the B-complex group.

Per serving:
Calories: 60
Sodium: 250 mg.

Protein: 1 g.
Fat: 4 g.
Carbohydrate: 6 g.

Right: Basic Italian Tomato Sauce, recipe page 126

COTTAGE PEAS

1 small onion, sliced
1 tablespoon margarine
10-ounce package frozen
  peas
½ teaspoon salt

¾ teaspoon curry powder
2 mint leaves, minced
1 cup cottage cheese
¼ teaspoon chili powder

Sauté onions in margarine until soft. Add peas, salt, curry, and mint. Cover and cook about 5 minutes, until peas are just tender. Remove from heat. Blend cottage cheese and chili powder together. Add to peas and mix thoroughly.

Serves 6

Nutrition Note: Peas are often among the few vegetables children will try, and they might really like these. Peas are packed with nutrition, providing a little protein along with vitamins A and B_3, iron, and potassium.

Per serving:
Calories: 152
Sodium: 825 mg.

Protein: 12 g.
Fat: 5 g.
Carbohydrate: 14 g.

1 pound fish fillets	3 tablespoons lemon juice
½ cup margarine	1 teaspoon honey
⅛ teaspoon garlic powder	1 teaspoon salt
2 teaspoons flour	⅛ teaspoon pepper
½ cup water	⅛ teaspoon poultry seasoning

Preheat oven to 350°F. In small saucepan, combine all ingredients except fish, stirring over low heat until bubbly. Remove and pour over fillets in a greased baking dish. Cover with foil and bake 20–30 minutes.

Serves 4

Nutrition Note: Try this dish on your "no fish wishers." It's nutritiously delicious and easy as 1,2,3 to fix.

Per serving:
Calories: 340
Sodium: 1,016 mg.

Protein: 24 g.
Fat: 24 g.
Carbohydrate: 6 g.

NEW ENGLAND BLUEFISH

2 large bluefish fillets
Butter
Salt

juice of 1 fresh lemon, or
white wine, or dry vermouth

Heat broiler. Grease and lightly salt the bottom of a pan large enough to hold the fillets in one layer with space between them. Dot tops of fillets with butter and sprinkle lightly with either lemon juice, white wine, or dry vermouth. Broil 4 inches from flame approximately 12–15 minutes until fish flakes easily.

Serves 4

Nutrition Note: A particularly moist and flavorful fish variety that even non-fish fans find they enjoy. It's low in saturated fats and a good source of phosphorus and protein.

Per serving:
Calories: 432
Sodium: 1,170 mg.

Protein: 29 g.
Fat: 28 g.
Carbohydrate: 8 g.

SURPRISE PACKAGE FISH

1 pound fish fillets
¼ cup butter or margarine
3 sprigs parsley
1 stalk celery, sliced
2 tablespoons Worcestershire
 sauce

½ teaspoon salt
1 teaspoon oregano
½ teaspoon basil
¼ teaspoon thyme
½ lemon, sliced thin

Preheat oven to 350°F. Cut fish into serving-size portions and place each on a foil square large enough to be folded over to enclose fish. Heat butter until melted. Add parsley, celery, Worcestershire sauce, salt, and herbs to melted butter, and stir. Pour some of this mixture over each serving, topping with a lemon slice. Fold foil into package and bake 30 minutes.

Fish is seldom a favorite with many children, but these silver packages take on the appealing appearance of little gifts to be unwrapped at dinnertime.

Serves 2–3

Per serving:
Calories: 447
Sodium: 3,850 mg.

Protein: 48 g.
Fat: 25 g.
Carbohydrate: 4 g.

2 pounds flounder or sole
  fillets
1 cup milk
Salt and pepper to taste
4 tablespoons margarine
½ tablespoon flour

½ cup light cream
2 tablespoons grated cheese
½ pound green seedless
  grapes or 1 cup chopped
  dried apricots
¼ cup wheat germ

Preheat oven to 400°F. In large skillet, simmer fish fillets in milk
5–10 minutes, according to thickness. Season with salt and pepper and remove carefully when done. Add margarine to stock
and slowly sprinkle in flour, stirring to thicken. Add cream and
cheese, simmering slowly until desired consistency is reached.
In buttered casserole dish, layer fish and fruit, and top with
sauce. Sprinkle with wheat germ and bake 15 minutes.

Serves 4

Nutrition Note: Nutritious and delicious, with just the right amount
of crunch. Calcium, iron, vitamins A and D are among the fruits
of this dish.

Per serving:	with grapes	with apricots
Calories:	520	634
Sodium:	319 mg.	333 mg.
Protein:	52 g.	54 g.
Fat:	23 g.	23 g.
Carbohydrate:	25 g.	54 g.

FRIED OYSTERS WITH LEMON BUTTER

2 7-ounce cans oysters
1 egg, beaten
1 tablespoon milk
¼ teaspoon salt
Dash of pepper
½ cup corn meal

½ cup oil
¼ cup butter or margarine
1 teaspoon lemon peel, grated
2 teaspoons fresh lemon juice
Dash of marjoram

Drain oysters. Combine egg, milk, salt, and pepper. Dip the oysters in this mixture and then roll in corn meal. Fry in hot oil, 2 or 3 minutes on each side until nicely browned. Drain. Melt the butter or margarine with the lemon peel and lemon juice, and season with marjoram. Serve the heated butter mixture with the fried oysters.

Serves 4

Nutrition Note: Oysters happen to be one of our major sources of iodine, though salt, in the iodized form, is probably our most common source.

Per serving:
Calories: 488
Sodium: 350 mg.

Protein: 10 g.
Fat: 42 g.
Carbohydrate: 18 g.

QUICK CRAB DINNER

10-ounce can condensed
  cream of shrimp soup
½ cup white wine
½ teaspoon Worcestershire
  sauce

½ cup sharp Cheddar
  cheese, grated
1 pound crab meat

In a saucepan, combine soup, wine, Worchestershire sauce, and cheese. Simmer until bubbly and smooth. Fold in crab meat gently and reheat. Serve over brown rice.

Serves 4

Per serving:
Calories: 298
Sodium: 1,860 mg.

Protein: 26 g.
Fat: 14 g.
Carbohydrate: 9 g.

1 chicken, quartered and skinned	1 cup honey
½ cup flour	2 tablespoons cornstarch
¼ teaspoon pepper	¾ cup vinegar
⅓ cup oil	1 tablespoon soy sauce
1 can sliced pineapple (1 pound, 4 ounces)	¼ teaspoon powdered ginger
	1 chicken bouillon cube
	1 large green pepper, sliced

Preheat oven to 350°F. Coat skinned chicken with combination of the flour and the pepper. Heat oil in large skillet and brown coated chicken. Drain on paper towels.

Dressing:

Drain pineapple, reserving fruit and pouring syrup into a 2-cup measure. Add enough water to make 1¼ cups. In saucepan, combine this liquid with honey, cornstarch, vinegar, soy sauce, ginger, and bouillon cube, and bring to a boil, stirring constantly for 2 minutes. Pour over chicken in baking dish and bake, uncovered, 30 minutes. Then place pineapple slices and green pepper strips on top and bake another 30 minutes. Serve with rice.

Serves 4

Nutrition Note: Take a culinary voyage to Hawaii tonight. A bouillon cube contains approximately 425 milligrams (mg.) of sodium —that's equivalent to just under ¼ teaspoon of salt.

Per serving: Protein: 16 g.
Calories: 485   Fat: 15 g.
Sodium: 330 mg.   Carbohydrate: 74 g.

1 cup celery, diced
1 onion, minced
1 tablespoon green pepper,
   minced
2 tablespoons flour
2 cups milk

1 chicken bouillon cube
   (optional)
1 can mushroom soup
3 cups cooked chicken, cubed
6 ounces wide noodles,
   cooked

Preheat oven to 375°F. Sauté the celery, onion, and pepper. Stir in flour, milk, bouillon cube, and soup, and simmer until thoroughly mixed. Fold in chicken cubes and noodles. Cover and bake for 30 minutes.

Serves 6

Nutrition Note: Another energy-efficient meal.

Per serving:
Calories: 399
Sodium: 706 mg.

Protein: 28 g.
Fat: 13 g.
Carbohydrate: 39 g.

BEER BATTER CHICKEN

1½ cups whole wheat flour
1 teaspoon salt
⅛ teaspoon pepper

1 can beer
1 frying chicken, quartered
   and skinned

Sift together flour, salt, and pepper. Mix with can of beer and set aside for 30 minutes. Wash chicken pieces and dry. Dip in batter. Fry in oil, covered, until done, and drain on paper towels.

Superb crust! Alcohol evaporates during cooking leaving only the flavor benefit.

Serves 4

Nutrition Note: Alcohol evaporates when used in cooking and only the flavor of the beer will remain.

Per serving:
Calories: 313
Sodium: 637 mg.

Protein: 26 g.
Fat: 5 g.
Carbohydrate: 36 g.

1 chicken, quartered
2 eggs
2 tablespoons grated
   Parmesan cheese
½ teaspoon parsley

1 teaspoon salt
¼ teaspoon pepper
1 cup bread crumbs
1-pound can tomato sauce
8 slices mozzarella cheese

Preheat oven to 350°F. Wash and dry chicken, and dip into mixture of eggs, cheese, parsley, and seasonings. Then cover with bread crumbs and sauté on both sides in hot oil until browned. Place in casserole dish and pour over tomato sauce. Bake 30 minutes; then open oven, top chicken with slices of mozzarella, and bake another 30 mintues.

Serves 4

Nutrition Note: A complete and balanced meal, providing protein, calcium, vitamins A and C, and members of the vitamin B-complex group. It's economical and energy-efficient, too!

Per serving:
Calories: 630
Sodium: 1,444 mg.

Protein: 47 g.
Fat: 35 g.
Carbohydrate: 32 g.

PEANUT PEACH SAUCE FOR CHICKEN

½ cup sliced peaches
   (or peach jam)
¼ cup heavy cream

¼ cup peanut butter
2 tablespoons soy sauce
1 tablespoon lemon juice

Puree in blender, heat in saucepan, and serve over broiled chicken.

Nutrition Note: Chicken never had it so good…nor did your picky eaters!

Per serving (1 oz):
Calories: 86
Sodium: 312 mg.

Protein: 2 g.
Fat: 7 g.
Carbohydrate: 5 g.

1 chicken, quartered	1 tablespoon flour
1 onion, minced	¼ cup white wine
2 carrots, diced	1 cube chicken bouillon
1 stalk celery, diced	Paprika to taste
½ teaspoon celery seed	⅛ teaspoon nutmeg
½ teaspoon onion powder	½ pound sliced mushrooms
8-ounce package	(optional)
spaghettini	1 cup milk
2 tablespoons margarine	½ cup Parmesan cheese

Simmer chicken in a large skillet in 3 cups of water with onion, carrots, celery, celery seed, and onion powder. Meanwhile simmer spaghettini in a separate pan until tender. Drain in a sieve. While the spaghettini drains, melt margarine, sprinkle in flour, and stir to a paste. Add wine, bouillon cube, 1 cup of the broth the chicken has been cooking in, paprika, nutmeg, and mushrooms. Cook and stir, slowly adding milk. Skin and bone the chicken pieces and combine chicken meat with sauce. Stir in the vegetables from the chicken broth and finally, the spaghettini. Before serving, top with grated cheese.

This is a treat the whole family will enjoy. Save the leftovers and reheat for lunch the next day!

Serves 4

Nutrition Note: A cost-effective approach to feeding "the troops," particularly appealing to today's parent on the go.

Per serving:
Calories: 525
Sodium: 345 mg.

Protein: 36 g.
Fat: 15 g.
Carbohydrate: 60 g.

1 chicken, whole or quartered	1 tablespoon grated orange rind
⅓ cup brown sugar	
⅓ cup honey	1 cup orange juice
1 tablespoon cornstarch	¼ teaspoon salt

Preheat oven to 350 °F. Combine ingredients other than chicken, stirring constantly, until liquid achieves a relatively thick consistency. Pour over chicken and bake 1 hour, basting if chicken is whole. Ten minutes before removing from the oven, decorate with fresh orange slices (or with canned mandarin slices).

Serves 4

Nutrition Note: A simple-to-make variation on plain old chicken, and a good source of vitamins B_1, B_2, B_3 (thiamine, riboflavin, and niacin), and B_{12}.

Per serving: Protein: 22 g.
Calories: 303   Fat: 3 g.
Sodium: 209 mg.   Carbohydrate: 49 g.

DIJON CHICKEN

3 slices good quality white bread	2 tablespoons oil
	3 chopped scallions
1 split broiler, lightly salted	¼ teaspoon thyme or basil
¾ of 8-ounce jar Dijon mustard	A few drops Tabasco (optional)

Preheat oven to 350 °F. Make bread crumbs by dropping one roughly torn slice at a time into a blender set at high speed. Empty blender after each slice. Set crumbs aside. Combine mustard, oil, scallions, thyme or basil, and Tabasco, and stir. Coat both sides of chicken with mustard mixture and roll in crumbs. Bake, uncovered on sheet, for 1 hour.

Serves 4

Nutrition Note: Low in saturated fat and high in protein.

Per serving: Protein: 56 g.
Calories: 608   Fat: 15 g.
Sodium: 1,493 mg.   Carbohydrate: 61 g.

German Cheese Dogs

Hot dog   Slice of pumpernickel bread
Slice of cheese

Cut a slit along the length of the hot dog up to ½ inch of either end. Stuff with cheese. Broil until cheese melts. Wrap bread around hot dog.

Per serving: Protein: 18 g.
Calories: 360   Fat: 24 g.
Sodium: 950 mg.   Carbohydrate: 18 g.

Dogs and Apple-Kraut

Hot dogs   Equal amounts of sauerkraut
                                        and applesauce

Drain the sauerkraut and mix with applesauce. Place in a long shallow pan to fit under the broiler. Top with hot dogs and broil 10 minutes, turning dogs half way through until crisp on both sides.

Per serving: Protein: 15 g.
Calories: 367   Fat: 26 g.
Sodium: 520 mg.   Carbohydrate: 19 g.

Pigs in a Blanket

1 package refrigerator   4 hot dogs, cut in half
   crescent rolls in dough form

Preheat oven to 375°F. Brown hot dog halves. Separate the dough as directed on the package. Lay one hot dog half on each triangle and roll dough around it. Bake 12 to 15 minutes on a cookie sheet.

Nutrition Note: Be sure to use all-beef frankfurters. And if you're interested in cutting down on fat and nitrites, go a step further and try chicken hot dogs in these recipes. They're available in the supermarket, alongside the traditional kind.

Per serving: Protein: 13 g.
Calories: 350   Fat: 15 g.
Sodium: 820 mg.   Carbohydrate: 39 g.

2 large sweet potatoes
1 cup apples, pared and sliced
½ pound all-beef frankfurters, sliced lengthwise
½ cup Cheddar cheese

⅛ cup brown sugar
¼ teaspoon salt
½ teaspoon lemon juice
½ cup bread crumbs
2 tablespoons butter, melted

Preheat oven to 375°F. Boil the sweet potatoes until soft, peel, and slice. Alternate layers of potatoes, apples, frankfurters, and cheese in casserole, using a total of half of each. Mix sugar and salt and sprinkle half on top of layers. Sprinkle on lemon juice. Add remaining layers of ingredients. Mix crumbs and butter and sprinkle on top. Bake 35 minutes.

Serves 4–6

Per serving:
Calories: 402
Sodium: 745 mg.

Protein: 12 g.
Fat: 20 g.
Carbohydrate: 42 g.

1 cup raisins	1 tablespoon vinegar
1½ cups water	¼ teaspoon each cinnamon,
⅓ cup brown sugar	dry mustard, salt
1½ teaspoons cornstarch	½ teaspoon powdered cloves

Boil raisins in water for 5 minutes. Combine sugar, cornstarch, and dry spices. Add to raisins. Cook, stirring until thickened. Blend in vinegar.

Makes 1½ cups

Serve hot on baked ham and garnish with pecans.

Nutrition Note: Raisins are a wonderful source of hard-to-get iron.

Per serving (2 tablespoons):	Protein: trace
Calories: 62	Fat: 0 g.
Sodium: 50 mg.	Carbohydrate: 16 g.

FRANKLY CORNY CASSEROLE

1 pound ground beef	2 cups milk
1 tablespoon minced onion	2 cups corn kernels, fresh
½ cup margarine	or frozen
3 tablespoons flour	12-ounce package corn
1 tablespoon dry mustard	bread mix
½ teaspoon salt	½ cup grated cheese

Preheat oven to 375°F. Sauté ground beef and onion in melted margarine. Blend flour, mustard, and salt, and add to the meat. Add milk and cook until thickened, stirring constantly. Add corn and pour into a greased casserole dish. Prepare corn bread batter according to package directions and drop batter by the tablespoonful around the edges of the casserole. Sprinkle grated cheese in the center and bake 30 minutes or until the corn bread is a golden brown.

Serves 4–6

Nutrition Note: Serve with a tossed green salad and a glass of fruit juice and you've got yourself a nutritious, easy-to-prepare family supper.

Per serving:	Protein: 26 g.
Calories: 660	Fat: 54 g.
Sodium: 854 mg.	Carbohydrate: 89 g.

STUFFED VEAL BREAST

4 or 5 pound veal breast	½ teaspoon poultry seasoning
1 teaspoon salt	2 tablespoons fresh parsley
1 cup raw brown rice	1 teaspoon grated orange
1 medium onion, chopped	rind
2 tablespoons oil	½ cup seedless raisins

Cut a large pocket in the veal breast side (or have your butcher do it). Wipe the veal with damp paper towels and set aside. Prepare brown rice, using ½ teaspoon of the salt, until just about tender. Remove from heat, drain, and let cool. Sauté chopped onion in oil until transparent and limp. In a bowl, combine the rice, onion, and all remaining ingredients. Stuff the veal breast pocket and close with a skewer or toothpicks. Place breast in a shallow roasting pan, rib side down, and brush with oil. Bake in 300°F oven for 2½ to 3 hours, or until tender, basting occasionally with pan liquid. Breast should be golden brown.

Serves 10

Nutrition Note: While not particularly economical, veal has a moderate fat content and is rich in iron, B vitamins, and protein.

Per serving:	Protein: 28 g.
Calories: 425	Fat: 24 g.
Sodium: 330 mg.	Carbohydrate: 21 g.

½ pound fresh pork sausage
3 onions, minced
1 tablespoon olive oil
4 carrots, peeled and
  chopped
2 stalks celery, chopped
3 ounces tomato paste

2 cups canned tomatoes
1½ teaspoons fennel seeds
½ teaspoon thyme
1½ teaspoons oregano
2 cloves garlic, minced
3 tablespoons Dijon mustard

Brown sausage, drain on paper towel. Wipe skillet. Sauté vegetables in oil, leaving carrots crunchy. Add sausage and remaining ingredients. Add water to desired degree of consistency and simmer 20 to 30 minutes. Serve over pasta or spaghetti squash.

Per 1 quart:
Calories: 1,670
Sodium: 2,846 mg.

Protein: 39 g.
Fat: 132 g.
Carbohydrate: 85 g.

Spaghetti Squash

This oval yellow summer squash has half the calories of spaghetti, which it resembles. To prepare, slice squash in half lengthwise and scoop out seeds. Bake halves face down on buttered tray in 375°F oven, about 45 minutes or until shell is easily pierced with fork. Top with sauce and cheese, as you would spaghetti.

CABBAGE AND MEATBALLS

1 small cabbage, shredded
2 large onions, sliced
2 carrots, peeled and chunked
¼ cup vinegar
2 tablespoons brown sugar
6-ounce can tomato paste
2 cups water
3 cloves

Dash of ginger
Salt and pepper to taste
1 pound ground beef
1 onion, grated
¼ cup raw rice
1 tablespoon parsley
Garlic powder to taste
1 egg, beaten

Grease a large skillet and sauté cabbage, onions, and carrots. When lightly glazed, add vinegar, brown sugar, tomato paste, water, and seasonings. Simmer, covered, for 30 minutes. Check occasionally to see if more water is needed.

To make meatballs, mix ground beef, onion, rice, seasonings, and egg. Roll into balls and sauté to brown. Add to the cabbage mixture and continue to simmer gently about 1 hour longer.

Note: Leftovers taste even better served the next day over rye bread!

Serves 4

Per serving:
Calories: 274
Sodium: 90 mg.

Protein: 20 g.
Fat: 8 g.
Carbohydrate: 29 g.

¾ pound ground beef
1 medium onion, minced
½ cup bread crumbs
1 egg, beaten
Salt and pepper to taste

2 large green peppers, cut in
    half sideways and cleaned
8-ounce can tomatoes
1 cup tomato sauce*
1 teaspoon oregano
Grated cheese

Preheat oven to 350°F. Mix beef, minced onion, bread crumbs, and beaten egg, seasoning to taste. Stuff mixture in green pepper cups carefully so as not to break them. Place in baking dish and pour tomatoes, sauce, and oregano around peppers. Top peppers with grated cheese and bake ½ hour. Serve on a bed of cooked brown rice.

Serves 4

Nutrition Note: Great way to beat inflation, the clock, and the absence of vegetables in many children's diets. They'll get plenty of protein and vitamin A in this dish.

*Why not keep some homemade tomato sauce, stored in 1-pint containers, in your freezer (see p. 126). If you're caught unprepared, choose a store-bought tomato sauce that contains no thickeners, additives, or extra salt.

Per serving:
Calories: 350
Sodium: 760 mg.

Protein: 27 g.
Fat: 17 g.
Carbohydrate: 22 g.

California Burger

Whole wheat pita bread
Thousand Island dressing
Bean sprouts
Monterey Jack cheese slices

Broiled hamburger
Shredded lettuce
Fresh tomato, chopped
Cucumber, chopped

Cut pita bread in half. Spread inside of one half with dressing. Line with sprouts and cheese. Slide in hamburger. Fill pocket with lettuce, tomato, and cucumber. Add more dressing if desired.

Per serving:
Calories: 510
Sodium: 500 mg.

Protein: 32 g.
Fat: 28 g.
Carbohydrate: 26 g.

Mushroom Burger

Sesame seed bun
Mayonnaise or ketchup
Fresh spinach leaves

Broiled hamburger
Fresh mushrooms, lightly
  sautéed

Lightly spread bun with mayonnaise or ketchup. Layer spinach, hamburger, and mushrooms. Close burger.

Per serving:
Calories: 485
Sodium: 540 mg.

Protein: 27 g.
Fat: 20 g.
Carbohydrate: 45 g.

Deli Burger

Broiled hamburger
Hard roll
Swiss cheese

Cole slaw
Red onion ring (optional)

Place hamburger on roll half. Top with Swiss cheese slice, cole slaw, and onion. Close burger.

Per serving:
Calories: 500
Sodium: 1,130 mg.

Protein: 34 g.
Fat: 20 g.
Carbohydrate: 40 g.

66   OVEN BEEF STEW

2 pounds chuck roast, cubed
2 8-ounce cans tomato sauce
1 cup celery, chunked
6 carrots, peeled and cut in
   large pieces
3 medium onions, sliced

2 tablespoons sugar
1 tablespoon salt
4 tablespoons tapioca
1 clove garlic, crushed
4 medium potatoes, cubed

Preheat oven to 250°F. Mix all the ingredients together in a large oven pan that has a cover. (No need to brown the meat!) Bake 5 to 6 hours until meat is tender.

This is a good stew to put together quickly at noon to simmer slowly for a hearty dinner.

Serves 4–6

Per serving:
Calories: 380
Sodium: 650 mg.

Protein: 18 g.
Fat: 19 g.
Carbohydrate: 34 g.

CHEESE-STUFFED FLANK STEAK

2 pounds flank steak
Oil and vinegar
1 medium onion, sliced thin
¼ pound mozzarella cheese

½ cup ricotta cheese*
Salt, pepper, and garlic
  powder to taste

Marinate the flank steak overnight in a mixture of 3 parts oil to 1 part vinegar. When ready to use, preheat oven to 350°F. Lay the steak flat and spread with a layer of onion slices, a layer of mozzarella, and a layer of ricotta. Season and roll. Skewer ends together and bake 1 hour.

Serves 4

Nutrition Note: Here's a dish rich in calcium, phosphorus, and B vitamins. Serve it with the children's favorite vegetable.

*Ricotta cheese is made from milk—either whole or skim. You might consider the skim milk variety, as it offers the richness and distinctive texture of ricotta cheese with less saturated fat and fewer calories.

Per serving:
Calories: 375
Sodium: 890 mg.

Protein: 36 g.
Fat: 23 g.
Carbohydrate: 4 g.

1 package pizza crust mix
1 can tomato sauce (tomato sauce sometimes comes with crust mix)
1 pound ground beef
1-pound can tomatoes
½ cup chopped mushrooms
½ cup sliced olives
Oregano to taste
Cheese (a mild yellow cheese is best)

Preheat oven to 350°F. Make crust according to package directions, patting it out in a greased 9x11-inch baking dish, covering bottom and sides. Spread tomato sauce over the dough. Sauté the ground beef and layer over sauce. Cut up the tomatoes and spread over meat. Layer mushrooms, olives, and oregano. Top with slices of cheese to cover. Bake for 45 minutes to 1 hour.

Serves 4

Per serving:
Calories: 305
Sodium: 635 mg.
Protein: 23 g.
Fat: 14 g.
Carbohydrate: 21 g.

LASAGNA

1 pound ground beef
2 large onions, minced
3 tablespoons oil
1 teaspoon salt
1½ teaspoons oregano
⅛ teaspoon pepper
Dash garlic salt
1 can tomatoes (1 pound, 12 ounces)
2 cans tomato sauce (8 ounces each)
1 pound lasagna noodles
1 pound ricotta cheese
8-ounce package mozzarella cheese
1 cup grated Parmesan cheese

Preheat oven to 350°F. Brown ground beef and onion in oil, adding seasonings. Simmer lasagna noodles according to package directions and drain, separating on paper towel. Grease a rectangular casserole dish and spread with combination of tomatoes and tomato sauce. Then lay strips of lasagna, ricotta, ground beef, and mozzarella, and repeat with layers of sauce, lasagna, ricotta, ground beef, and mozzarella. Top with grated Parmesan and bake 50 minutes.

Serves 6

Per serving:	with meat	meatless
Calories:	633	532
Sodium:	940 mg.	900 mg.
Protein:	38 g.	27 g.
Fat:	28 g.	22 g.
Carbohydrate:	54 g.	54 g.

1½ pounds ground beef
1 onion, diced
2 tablespoons mustard
1 tablespoon vinegar

¾ cup Ketchup
  (see p. 124)
1 can cream of celery soup

Sauté meat and onions. Add remaining ingredients and simmer 30 minutes.

Note: Kids will pressure you for Sloppy Joes. Serve them over a good bread. Whole wheat English muffins can be just as much fun as hamburger rolls, and they are more nutritious.

Makes 6–8

Per serving:
Calories: 200
Sodium: 460 mg.

Protein: 19 g.
Fat: 10 g.
Carbohydrate: 7 g.

½ leg of lamb
6 tablespoons lemon juice
4 tablespoons oil
2 tablespoons grated onion
1 teaspoon ginger
½ teaspoon pepper
Shake of garlic salt

2 teaspoons curry powder
1 teaspoon salt
18 mushroom caps
2 green peppers, cut into
    1-inch squares
24 pineapple chunks

Cut lamb into 1-inch cubes. Marinate for 6 hours more or less in a mixture of the next 8 ingredients. On 6 skewers, alternate chunks of lamb with mushrooms, pineapple, and green peppers. Broil 5–10 minutes.

Serves 6

Nutrition Note: A mouth-watering way to expand the kids' culinary horizons, with fruits and vegetables built right in.

Per serving: Protein: 13 g.
Calories: 288   Fat: 20 g.
Sodium: 430 mg.   Carbohydrate: 16 g.

Left: Country Baked Beans, recipe page 28

SAUTÉED NECTARINES AND LAMB CHOPS

2 tablespoons butter
2 tablespoons brown sugar
Lemon juice

4 unpeeled nectarines,
    sliced and pitted
4 lamp chops

Heat butter and brown sugar until bubbling. Add nectarines and simmer until glazed. Sprinkle lightly with lemon juice. Serve with broiled lamp chops.

Serves 4

Per serving: Protein: 15 g.
Calories: 308   Fat: 14 g.
Sodium: 125 mg.   Carbohydrate: 27 g.

½ cup shortening
1 cup sugar
2 eggs
2 cups flour
1 teaspoon baking soda
2 tablespoons buttermilk or
  sour milk

½ teaspoon salt
1 teaspoon vanilla extract
2 cups apples, pared,
  cored, and chopped,
  but not too small

Preheat oven to 325°F. Mix ingredients together and bake in a greased loaf pan for 1 hour.

Topping (optional):

4 teaspoons sugar   1 teaspoon cinnamon

Mix the sugar and cinnamon and sprinkle on top of bread before baking.

1 loaf

Nutrition Note: Try substituting some whole wheat flour in a recipe that calls for flour—a ratio of 2 to 1 is usually safe (e.g., in a recipe calling for 1 cup of flour, use ⅓ cup whole wheat flour and ⅔ cup regular flour). You may enjoy the resulting texture and slightly nutty flavor, and the added dietary fiber is a benefit.

Per loaf:
Calories: 2,050
Sodium: 2,440 mg.

Protein: 22 g.
Fat: 125 g.
Carbohydrate: 245 g.

BANANA BREAD

⅓ cup margarine
1 cup dark brown sugar
2 eggs
2 mashed bananas
   (about 1 cup)

1 ¾ cups flour
2 teaspoons baking powder
¼ teaspoon baking soda
½ teaspoon salt
½ cup chopped walnuts

Preheat oven to 350°F. Beat margarine and slowly add sugar until fluffy. Add egg and bananas, continuing to beat. Sift dry ingredients and mix into batter until creamy. Add nuts. Pour batter into a greased 5x9-inch loaf pan and bake 45 minutes to 1 hour, until firm and nicely browned. Do not slice until cool.

This is a perfect way to use bananas that are beginning to spot. It makes a delicious lunchbox treat, especially spread with peanut butter.

1 loaf

Nutrition Note: Loaded with B vitamins, potassium, and some vitamin A.

Per loaf:
Calories: 2,925
Sodium: 3,125 mg.

Protein: 49 g.
Fat: 115 g.
Carbohydrate: 435 g.

BOSTON BROWN BREAD

1 cup raisins
1½ cups water
1 egg
1 cup light brown sugar
1 tablespoon margarine,
   softened

1 cup orange juice
2 cups flour
1 teaspoon baking soda
½ teaspoon salt
4 empty, cleaned and greased
   10½-ounce soup cans

Preheat oven to 350°F. Boil raisins in water about 5 minutes and drain. Beat together the egg, sugar, and margarine. Stir flour, baking soda, and salt together. Add juice and flour alternately to batter, continuing to beat as you do. Add raisins. Bake in cans about 45 minutes.

Everybody gets his or her own little bread circle. For a real treat, top with whipped cream.

4 small loaves

Nutrition Note: An excellent source of iron. Can be used to make a healthy peanut butter and banana sandwich for the lunch box or an after-school snack. Don't forget about combining this bread with Country-Style Baked Beans (p. 28).

Per loaf:
Calories: 595
Sodium: 510 mg.

Protein: 9 g.
Fat: 5 g.
Carbohydrate: 130 g.

HERB BREAD

1 package yeast
¼ cup warm water
¾ cup milk, scalded
2 tablespoons shortening
2 tablespoons sugar
1½ teaspoons salt

3 full cups whole wheat flour
2 teaspoons celery seed
1 teaspoon ground sage
½ teaspoon nutmeg
1 egg, beaten

Soften yeast in water until it is active (bubbly). Combine scalded milk, shortening, sugar, and salt, and cool to lukewarm. Add about half of the flour, stirring well. Add seasonings, active yeast, and egg. Beat until smooth. Add remaining flour (or enough to make moderately soft dough). Turn out on lightly floured surface; cover and let rest 10 minutes. Then knead the dough until smooth and elastic, about 8 minutes. Place in a lightly greased bowl, turning once to grease surface. Cover. Let rise in a warm place until double in bulk. (It is a good idea to put the bowl in a pan of hot water on the lower rack of the oven.) This process should take about 1½ hours. Punch down; let rest 10–15 minutes. Shape into a round loaf and place on greased baking sheet. Cover. Let rise in a warm place until double again (about an hour). Bake in 400°F oven for 35 minutes, or until done.

Note: To glaze the top, beat an egg white slightly, brush it over surface of loaf, and sprinkle with celery seed before baking.

1 loaf

Per loaf:
Calories: 1,800
Sodium: 3,825 mg.

Protein: 63 g.
Fat: 47 g.
Carbohydrate: 290 g.

2 packages yeast	5½ cups flour, sifted
¼ cup lukewarm water	2 eggs
1 cup milk	½ cup chopped citron
¼ cup sugar	½ cup raisins
1½ teaspoons salt	½ cup chopped nuts
½ cup shortening	

Soften yeast in warm water until active (bubbly). Meanwhile, scald milk, adding sugar, salt, and shortening. Cool to lukewarm. Beat 2 cups of the flour into milk mixture, then stir in yeast and eggs. Stir in remaining ingredients, including the rest of the flour. Turn out and knead until smooth. Place in a greased bowl and cover, letting dough rise until double in bulk. Divide the dough in half. Shape each portion into a greased loaf pan. Allow dough to double again. Bake for 35–40 minutes in preheated 375°F oven.

2 loaves

Per loaf:	Protein: 51 g.
Calories: 2,265	Fat: 86 g.
Sodium: 2,045 mg.	Carbohydrate: 320 g.

IRISH SODA BREAD

2 tablespoons oil	1 teaspoon baking soda
2 tablespoons white vinegar	½ teaspoon salt
1½ cups milk	2 tablespoons caraway seeds
2 tablespoons honey	1 cup raisins
3½ cups flour	

Preheat oven to 350°F. Place oil and vinegar in measuring cup and fill to 1-cup level with milk. Pour into mixing bowl and add an additional ¾ cup milk. Add honey and stir. Let the mixture thicken while measuring and mixing the dry ingredients. Combine dry ingredients and liquid. Bake 45 minutes to 1 hour in a greased and floured loaf pan. After removing bread, rub with melted butter.

1 loaf

Per loaf:
Calories: 2,475
Sodium: 1,735 mg.

Protein: 57 g.
Fat: 46 g.
Carbohydrate: 459 g.

1 egg
¼ cup sugar
½ cup shortening
1 cup milk

2 cups flour
1 teaspoon salt
3 teaspoons baking powder
1 cup fresh blueberries

Preheat oven to 400°F. Mix egg, sugar, and shortening. Add milk, flour, salt, and baking powder. Fold in blueberries. Bake approximately 25 minutes in greased muffin tins.

Makes 12

Per muffin:
Calories: 190
Sodium: 295 mg.

Protein: 4 g.
Fat: 10 g.
Carbohydrate: 20 g.

RAISIN BRAN MUFFINS

1 ¼ cups whole wheat flour
2 cups raisin bran flakes
¾ cup sugar
1 ¼ teaspoons salt
1 teaspoon vinegar

1 cup milk
¼ cup oil
1 egg
¾ cup raisins

Preheat oven to 400°F. Mix flour, bran flakes, sugar, and salt. Drop vinegar into milk to sour (or use 1 cup buttermilk) and add oil and egg. Mix dry with liquid ingredients and beat until blended. Add raisins. Bake 15 minutes.

These muffins can be stored in a sealed container in the refrigerator for a few weeks. To serve, pop into a toaster oven or heat in the oven.

Makes 12

Nutrition Note: Each muffin is a potent package of nutrition: iron, B vitamins, protein, and fiber.

Per muffin:
Calories: 208
Sodium: 280 mg.

Protein: 4 g.
Fat: 6 g.
Carbohydrate: 35 g.

2 cups whole wheat pastry flour (plain whole wheat flour can be used but pastry flour turns out a more tender biscuit)
2 teaspoons baking powder

½ teaspoon salt
¼ teaspoon baking soda
¾ cup buttermilk (or milk with a teaspoon of vinegar added to sour it)

Preheat oven to 425°F. Toss ingredients together and knead until no longer sticky. Do not knead too much—the less you knead, the flakier the biscuit. Roll dough with floured rolling pin to ¾-inch thickness. Cut with floured biscuit cutter or top of a small glass.

For Biscuits: Bake about 15 minutes.

For Doughnuts: Flatten dough with rolling pin until about ½ inch thick. Cut into 12 doughnuts, using a doughnut cutter, a biscuit cutter, or a small glass—if you use a biscuit cutter or a glass, make the doughnut holes using a bottle cap. Heat oil in skillet to approximately 350°F. Drop each doughnut into the oil and turn when it browns. Sprinkle each doughnut with confectioner's sugar and cinnamon while still hot.

Makes 12

Nutrition Note: Serve these biscuits at a weekend breakfast with yogurt and a fresh fruit salad.

Per serving:	per biscuit	per doughnut
Calories:	72	122
Sodium:	185 mg.	185 mg.
Protein:	2 g.	2 g.
Fat:	trace	5 g.
Carbohydrate:	15 g.	15 g.

3 ounces cream cheese
½ cup margarine
¼ cup sugar
1½ cups flour

Confectioner's sugar
Cherries, pitted and sliced
   in half, or walnuts, for
   decoration (optional)

Mix the cream cheese, margarine, and sugar together to soften. Add flour and blend. Form into small balls and place half a cherry or a walnut on top of each. Bake on greased cookie sheet at 400°F for 10–15 minutes, until browned. Sprinkle confectioner's sugar on top while still warm from the oven.

Makes about 1 dozen

Per cookie:
Calories: 190
Sodium: 110 mg.

Protein: 2 g.
Fat: 10 g.
Carbohydrate: 22 g.

Far right: Pumpkin Date Cookies, recipe page 81
Bottom left: Nut Cookies, recipe page 80

½ cup margarine
1 cup brown sugar
1 egg yolk
Pinch of salt
1 teaspoon vanilla extract

2 cups flour
½ cup shortening
1 teaspoon baking soda
1 egg white, beaten lightly
½ cup nuts, chopped

Preheat oven to 325°F. Mix first 8 ingredients in order given, and place mixture in greased baking tin. Spread beaten egg white over batter and sprinkle chopped nuts on top. Bake for 40 minutes. Cut into squares as soon as you remove pan from oven.

Makes 12 squares

Per square:
Calories: 325
Sodium: 175 mg.

Protein: 3 g.
Fat: 21 g.
Carbohydrate: 32 g.

Far left: Cream Cheese Cookies, recipe page 79
Middle: Nut Cookies, recipe page 80
Far right: Pumpkin Date Cookies, recipe page 81
Top right: Parsnip Bake, recipe page 46
Middle left: Finland Whipped Cream Fruit Cake, recipe page 100

½ cup margarine
¾ cup brown sugar
1 egg, lightly beaten
1½ teaspoons vanilla extract
Pinch of salt
½ cup whole wheat flour

¾ teaspoon baking powder
1 cup wheat germ
1½ cups rolled oats
¾ cup raisins
½ cup chopped nuts

Preheat oven to 375°F. Cream together margarine, sugar, egg, vanilla, and salt. Beat. Stir dry ingredients together and blend with margarine mixture, adding water by the teaspoon if needed for proper consistency. Place on greased cookie sheet by teaspoonfuls and bake 10–12 minutes.

Here's a cookie that is also good for you!

Makes 2 dozen

Nutrition Note: These cookies are little energy packages, full of B vitamins, iron, phosphorus and fiber.

Per cookie:
Calories: 155
Sodium: 60 mg.

Protein: 4 g.
Fat: 7 g.
Carbohydrate: 19 g.

PUMPKIN DATE COOKIES

1¼ cups flour, sifted
1½ teaspoons salt
1 teaspoon baking powder
¼ teaspoon baking soda
¾ cup oatmeal
½ cup shortening
1 cup brown sugar

¾ cup white sugar
1 teaspoon cinnamon
½ teaspoon nutmeg
1 egg
1 cup pumpkin, cooked
1 cup dates, chopped
¾ cup walnuts, chopped

Preheat oven to 375°F. Mix flour, salt, baking powder, and baking soda. Stir in oatmeal. Cream the shortening, sugars, and spices. Beat in the egg and then the pumpkin. Slowly mix in the dry ingredients. Fold in dates and walnuts. Drop by tablespoonfuls on greased cookie sheets. Bake 15 minutes.

Makes 3 dozen

Nutrition Note: Not just for Halloween, make these cookies often and spread the wealth; they're rich in vitamin A and iron.

Per cookie:
Calories: 125
Sodium: 115 mg.

Protein: 1 g.
Fat: 5 g.
Carbohydrate: 19 g.

Top right: Whole Wheat Biscuits or Doughnuts, recipe page 78
Top left: Blueberry Muffins, recipe page 77

84 AVOCADO-SLAW

1 cup shredded cabbage	Lemon juice to taste
⅓ cup mayonnaise	Salt to taste
4 slices dark bread	4 tomato slices
1 small avocado	

Mix cabbage and mayonnaise. Spread a layer of this slaw mix on the bread. Add a slice of avocado, squeeze lemon juice on top, and salt to taste. Top with a tomato slice.

Note: This filling can also be tucked into pita bread.

Makes 4 open sandwiches

Nutrition Note: Supplement this sandwich with a stick of the children's favorite cheese and a cold, crisp apple for a balanced meal that supplies vitamin A, calcium, and protein.

Per sandwich:	Protein: 7 g.
Calories: 350	Fat: 24 g.
Sodium: 675 mg.	Carbohydrate: 30 g.

DEVILED EGGS

3 hard-boiled eggs
⅛ cup mayonnaise
½ teaspoon vinegar

1 teaspoon dry mustard
⅛ teaspoon salt
Dash pepper

Halve eggs lengthwise. Remove yolks and place them in a small bowl. Mash yolks thoroughly with other ingredients. Refill egg whites with yolk mixture and wrap in foil for the lunchbox.

Makes 6

Per serving (2):
Calories: 149
Sodium: 215 mg.

Protein: 7 g.
Fat: 13 g.
Carbohydrate: 0 g.

EGG SALAD

Hard-boiled eggs
Chopped celery
Sliced fresh mushrooms
Minced green pepper

Wheat germ or sesame seeds
Minced avocado
Minced onion

Dressing:

Mayonnaise (4 parts) and
lemon juice (1 part)

Salt and pepper to taste

The quantities should be adjusted to taste and availability. Ingredients, other than eggs and dressing, are optional.

Nutrition Note: Serve on 7-grain bread or in a pita bread half, and add tomato slices, cucumbers, and fresh spinach leaves for a nutritious, California-style lunch treat.

Per sandwich:
Calories: 425
Sodium: 705 mg.

Protein: 20 g.
Fat: 22 g.
Carbohydrate: 39 g.

PEANUT BUTTER-BANANA

Margarine
Creamy peanut butter

Banana slices

Between slices of bread, spread margarine, creamy peanut butter, and banana slices.

This simple sandwich must rate as a lunchbox classic. Don't be put off by its simplicity—it is also nourishing!

Per sandwich:
Calories: 400
Sodium: 360 mg.

Protein: 14 g.
Fat: 21 g.
Carbohydrate: 46 g.

COTTAGE CHEESE-APRICOT

Mayonnaise
Lettuce leaves
Cottage cheese

Chopped dried apricots
Chopped nuts

Spread bread with layer of mayonnaise and lettuce leaves. Mix cottage cheese, chopped apricots, and nuts, and spread.

Nutrition Note: If you can get the kids to like this sandwich filling, you've added a wonderful source of iron, calcium, phosphorus, and protein to their diets. Of course, spread it between slices of whole grain bread.

Per sandwich:
Calories: 450
Sodium: 485 mg.

Protein: 15 g.
Fat: 15 g.
Carbohydrate: 63 g.

Left: Peach Chicken Salad, recipe page 37

10½-ounce can minced clams
8 ounces cream cheese
½ teaspoon soy sauce
½ teaspoon lemon juice
½ teaspoon clam juice
Hot pepper sauce to taste

Drain the minced clams, reserving ½ teaspoon liquid. Blend all ingredients and store in refrigerator in a capped bottle for use as a sandwich spread. When ready to use, simply spread over bread.

Per sandwich:
Calories: 250
Sodium: 380 mg.
Protein: 10 g.
Fat: 12 g.
Carbohydrate: 26 g.

SALMON-CHEESE

1 large can salmon
8 ounces cream cheese
1 teaspoon Worcestershire sauce
1 teaspoon horseradish
2 teaspoons grated onion
¼ teaspoon salt
Dash pepper
1 teaspoon lemon juice
3 tablespoons parsley flakes
½ cup chopped nuts

Thoroughly mix all ingredients and store in refrigerator in clean, capped jar to use for sandwich spread.

Per serving:	per recipe mixture	per sandwich
Calories:	1,214	220
Sodium:	3,220 mg.	580 mg.
Protein:	100 g.	17 g.
Fat:	80 g.	13 g.
Carbohydrate:	22 g.	8 g.

Left: Mariner's Macaroni, recipe page 37

DEEP-SEA SALAD

Mayonnaise
Lemon juice
Salt
Pepper

Equal-size cans of any
   combination of:
   tuna, salmon, shrimp,
   crab
Minced onion
Minced celery

Depending on the quantity you are preparing, mix portions of mayonnaise and lemon juice in quantities of about 4 parts mayonnaise to 1 part lemon juice, or to suit desired tartness. Add salt and pepper to taste. Drain fish, and combine with onion and celery. Toss fish with mayonnaise mixture, and serve over lettuce leaves as a salad or spread on bread for a sandwich.

Nutrition Note: Serve on dark rye or whole wheat English muffins.

Per recipe:
Calories: 2,095
Sodium: 4,700 mg.

Protein: 82 g.
Fat: 194 g.
Carbohydrate: 8 g.

CURRY-TUNA HOT SANDWICH

7-ounce can tuna
½ cup celery, chopped
¼ cup almonds, chopped

½ cup shredded coconut
½ cup mayonnaise
½ teaspoon curry powder

Heat broiler. Drain tuna and mix with remaining ingredients. Spread on buttered bread. Broil 3 or 4 inches from heat for 2–3 minutes until lightly browned.

Serves 4

Nutrition Note: Slightly crunchy, subtly sweet, it makes already nutritious tuna a special treat!

Per sandwich:
Calories: 750
Sodium: 830 mg.

Protein: 28 g.
Fat: 67 g.
Carbohydrate: 12 g.

2 hard-boiled eggs,
    coarsely chopped
1 tablespoon lemon juice
½ cup mayonnaise

¼ cup sliced sweet pickle
1 tablespoon chopped onion
¼ teaspoon salt
6½-ounce can tuna, drained

Thoroughly mix all ingredients, adding tuna last. Serve on sandwich bread with lettuce leaves and tomato slices.

Per sandwich:
Calories: 385
Sodium: 740 mg.

Protein: 17 g.
Fat: 29 g.
Carbohydrate: 15 g.

JIFFY APPLE NUT BAKE

1 teaspoon baking powder
½ cup honey
¼ cup brown sugar
2 tablespoons whole wheat
    flour

1 well-beaten egg
3 unpeeled apples, washed,
    cored, and sliced in eighths
½ cup walnuts, chopped

Preheat oven to 350°F. Mix baking powder, honey, sugar, flour, and egg thoroughly. Add apples and nuts and bake 50 minutes in greased 1-quart pan.

Here's a pie without the bother of making a pie crust!

Serves 4–6

Per recipe:
Calories: 250
Sodium: 57 mg.

Protein: 29 g.
Fat: 7 g.
Carbohydrate: 459 g.

APPLESAUCE CAKE

½ cup shortening
1¼ cups sugar
2 cups applesauce
1 egg, beaten
3 cups flour
½ teaspoon salt

2 teaspoons baking soda
2 teaspoons cinnamon
½ teaspoon allspice
¼ teaspoon cloves
5 ounces raisins or mixed
    dried fruit or nuts

Preheat oven to 325°F. Cream together shortening, sugar, applesauce, and egg. Sift the flour with other dry ingredients and stir. Combine with liquid, and mix in raisins. Bake in greased pans for 1 hour or more.

1 large tube cake or 2 loaves

Nutrition Note: Apples, raisins, and nuts give this confection its redeeming nutritional value.

Per recipe:
Calories: 3,940
Sodium: 2,445 mg.

Protein: 12 g.
Fat: 125 g.
Carbohydrate: 693 g.

⅔ cup sugar
¼ cup flour
½ teaspoon cinnamon
3 cups fresh blueberries

Whole Wheat Crumb Crust
 (see p. 125)
1 tablespoon margarine

Preheat oven to 425°F. Mix sugar, flour, and cinnamon, and stir into the blueberries. Place the mix into the crust and dot with margarine. Bake for 35–45 minutes.

Per serving (⅛ pie):
Calories: 275
Sodium: 165 mg.

Protein: 5 g.
Fat: 10 g.
Carbohydrate: 40 g.

Right: Blueberry Muffins, recipe page 77

BLUEBERRY CREAM PIE

1 package vanilla pudding mix
1½ cups milk
½ pint heavy cream, whipped
Whole Wheat Crumb Crust
 (see p. 125)

2 cups blueberries
1 tablespoon lemon juice
1 tablespoon cornstarch
2 tablespoons sugar
1 tablespoon margarine

Bring pudding mix and milk to full boil, cool, and add whipped cream, reserving some for topping. Pour into crumb-lined pie shell. Simmer blueberries, lemon juice, cornstarch, and sugar in a saucepan until thick and clear. Stir in margarine and cool. Spoon over pudding mixture. Top with whipped cream.

Per serving (⅛ pie):
Calories: 386
Sodium: 260 mg.

Protein: 7 g.
Fat: 23 g.
Carbohydrate: 38 g.

BREAD PUDDING

⅔ cups honey	2 cups dry whole wheat
1 tablespoon margarine	bread cubes
½ teaspoon salt	4 eggs, lightly beaten
1 teaspoon vanilla extract	½ cup raisins
4 cups hot milk	½ cup nuts, chopped

Preheat oven to 350°F. Stir honey, margarine, salt, and vanilla into hot milk and pour over bread cubes. Stir in beaten eggs and mix in raisins and nuts. Grease a 1½-quart baking dish and pour in mixture. Place baking dish in a larger pan containing enough water to come halfway up the sides of the baking dish and bake pudding for about 1 hour or until firm. Serve pudding topped with whipped cream, yogurt, or milk.

Serves 4–6

Nutrition Note: Kids who won't drink their milk will get their share of calcium and protein in this dessert or snack—with the bonus of iron, phosphorus, and extra protein from the eggs.

Per serving:	Protein: 12 g.
Calories: 435	Fat: 18 g.
Sodium: 390 mg.	Carbohydrate: 55 g.

1 cup grated carrots
1 cup raisins
¾ cup honey
1 teaspoon salt
1 teaspoon cinnamon
1 teaspoon allspice
½ teaspoon nutmeg

¼ teaspoon cloves
1 tablespoon margarine
1½ cups water
1½ cups whole wheat flour
1 teaspoon baking soda
½ cup wheat germ

Icing

½ box confectioner's sugar
½ stick margarine or butter,
  softened

1 tablespoon milk
1 teaspoon vanilla extract
½ cup walnuts, chopped

Cake: Preheat oven to 350°F. Cook carrots, raisins, honey, salt, spices, and margarine in the water for 10 minutes. Allow to cool, while mixing together flour, baking soda, and wheat germ. Combine and stir, pouring into well-greased loaf pan. Bake 45 minutes.

Icing: Beat sugar, margarine or butter, milk, and vanilla to a nice consistency for icing, adding more sugar if needed. Stir in walnuts.

Note: Some kids love their carrot cake plain, and you can omit the sugary icing.

Nutrition Note: Classically nutritious, delicious, and fattening.

Per loaf:
Calories: 4,200
Sodium: 2,260 mg.

Protein: 65 g.
Fat: 109 g.
Carbohydrate: 740 g.

Bottom, far right: Herb Bread, recipe page 74
Bottom, far left: Applesauce Cake, recipe page 92
Bottom, middle: Banana Bread, recipe page 73
Top: Parsnip Bake, recipe page 46

2 cups Whole Wheat Crumb
    Crust mixture (see p. 125)
½ cup melted margarine or
    butter
½ cup walnuts, chopped fine
1 pound cream cheese
1 pint sour cream

3 eggs
½ teaspoon salt
1 teaspoon almond extract
1 cup sugar
Fresh blueberries,
    strawberries, raspberries,
    or bananas (optional)

Preheat oven to 350°F. Mix crumbs, margarine or butter, and walnuts, and press on bottom of spring-form pan. Beat the rest of the ingredients, except fruit, until smooth, pour over crumbs, and bake 35 minutes. Chill for 6 hours before serving. Top with choice of fruit, or serve plain.

Nutrition Note: This one is loaded...especially with calories, but has its share of calcium, vitamins, and pleasure, too!

Per serving (1/12 cake):
Calories: 505
Sodium: 415 mg.

Protein: 10 g.
Fat: 39 g.
Carbohydrate: 28 g.

1 tablespoon margarine
6 ounces milk chocolate
½ cup evaporated milk
1 teaspoon instant coffee

Sliced banana
Orange segments
Pineapple chunks
Apple wedges

Melt margarine, chocolate, and milk over low heat, and stir in coffee. Pour this mixture into a chafing dish. Each person gets a dish of fruit and a skewer. Skewer the fruit and dip into the warm chocolate mixture, holding it a while before eating until cooled slightly.

This is a make-your-own-piece-of-candy dish that is fun, and, all in all, is relatively healthful!

Per recipe:
Calories: 1,460
Sodium: 400 mg.

Protein: 20 g.
Fat: 74 g.
Carbohydrate: 180 g.

CRANBERRY CAKE

½ cup plus 1 tablespoon
   shortening
1 cup sugar
¼ teaspoon almond extract
1 egg, beaten
2 cups flour
½ teaspoon salt
1 teaspoon baking soda

1¼ teaspoons baking powder
1 teaspoon cinnamon
¼ teaspoon cloves
¼ teaspoon ground allspice
1 cup raisins, soaked and
   drained
1-pound can whole cranberry
   sauce

Preheat oven to 350°F. Cream shortening and sugar. Add almond extract to beaten egg and then to sugar mixture. Sift together dry ingredients and blend with mixture, folding in raisins and cranberry sauce. Pour into a greased 9-inch tube pan and bake for 1 hour or until done.

Nutrition Note: Cranberries are among nature's wonderful and versatile sources of vitamin C.

Per recipe:
Calories: 3,810
Sodium: 2,020 mg.

Protein: 34 g.
Fat: 115 g.
Carbohydrate: 660 g.

CUSTARD

3 eggs	Salt to taste
¼ cup honey	Raisins (optional)
1 teaspoon vanilla extract	Sliced fruit (optional)
2 cups milk, warmed	Chopped nuts (optional)

Preheat oven to 325°F. Beat eggs, honey, and vanilla, gradually adding warm milk. Stir in few shakes of salt. Pour into custard cups or small casserole. Add a total of about ¾ to 1 cup of any of the optional ingredients, and bake 50 minutes or until a knife inserted in the center comes out clean.

Serves 4

Nutrition Note: Another realistic substitute for milk. Raisins, fruits, and nuts make this already nutritious food that much more valuable. You might serve the fruited version for breakfast.

Per serving: Protein: 9 g.
Calories: 210   Fat: 9 g.
Sodium: 180 mg.   Carbohydrate: 22 g.

Left: Mixed Fruit and Sweetened Cream, recipe page 113

CREAM PUFFS

½ cup shortening	1 cup flour
1 cup boiling water	4 eggs

Preheat oven to 400°F. In a saucepan, add the shortening to the boiling water and bring to a boil again. Add flour all at once and stir rapidly. Mixture will form into a stiff and smooth ball of dough which will leave the sides of the pan clean. Cool, then add eggs, one at a time, beating well after each addition. Drop by spoonfuls on a greased pan about 2 inches apart, shaping each into a ball. Bake 30 minutes, the first 10 minutes in a 400° oven and then reducing to 350°. Take one out; if it doesn't fall, the others can be removed, if it does collapse, check remaining puffs at 2-minute intervals until done. Cool. Slice. Fill with your favorite filling or see Creamed Fruit, p. 112.

Makes 12

Per serving: Protein: 6 g.
Calories: 220   Fat: 12 g.
Sodium: 140 mg.   Carbohydrate: 16 g.

FRESH FRUIT COFFEE CAKE 99

¼ pound butter or margarine
2 eggs
1 teaspoon vanilla extract
1 cup sugar
1 cup sour cream
2 cups whole wheat flour

1 teaspoon baking powder
1 teaspoon baking soda
½ teaspoon salt
Fresh blueberries,
    sliced peaches,
    or diced apples

Preheat oven to 350°F. Cream first 5 ingredients in mixer. Slowly add remaining dry ingredients. Fold in fruit. Bake in greased 2-quart pan for 50 minutes.

Per recipe:
Calories: 3,125
Sodium: 3,165 mg.

Protein: 51 g.
Fat: 147 g.
Carbohydrate: 400 g.

NO-NEED-TO-BAKE FRESH FRUIT PIE

1 tablespoon margarine
½ cup wheat germ
4 cups fresh fruit (peaches,
    bananas, blueberries,
    raspberries, or any one of
    these fruits by itself or in
    combinations. Peaches are
    particularly good!)

2 cups milk
2 tablespoons cornstarch
½ cup brown sugar
½ teaspoon salt
1 teaspoon vanilla extract
¼ cup nuts
¼ cup shredded coconut

Grease 10-inch pie plate with margarine and sprinkle layer of wheat germ around bottom and sides. Top with fruit. Place milk, cornstarch, brown sugar, salt, and vanilla in saucepan, and cook slowly until thickened. Pour over fruit. Sprinkle top with mixture of additional wheat germ, nuts, and coconut. Chill.

If you want a more sturdy crust, substitute Whole Wheat Crumb Crust (see p. 125).

Nutrition Note: This has to be, without doubt, the richest pie in vitamins and fiber that you've ever tried.

Per serving (⅛ pie):
Calories: 255
Sodium: 200 mg.

Protein: 5 g.
Fat: 8 g.
Carbohydrate: 40 g.

4 eggs
Sugar
Whole wheat flour
1 teaspoon baking powder
¾ cup orange or pineapple
  juice
3 large bananas

Berries in season
  (strawberries, blueberries,
  raspberries, etc.)
1 pint heavy cream
Vanilla extract and sugar
  to taste

Preheat oven to 375°F. Crack eggs into a glass. In an additional glass, pour equal amount of sugar. Transfer sugar to mixing bowl. Measure in empty glass the same amount of whole wheat flour. Mix baking powder into it. Whip together eggs and sugar, slowly sprinkling flour mixture in while whipping. Pour into well-greased cake pan and bake 15 minutes, or until set. Just before serving, pour juice over cake. Mash 2 bananas and about a cup of berries together and spread over top. Whip heavy cream, adding about a teaspoon vanilla and about a teaspoon sugar, and cover the fruit with it. Decorate with slices of remaining banana and additional berries.

A Manhattan mother reports her Finnish house-helper made this recipe several years in a row as a birthday cake and it is now a family staple on holidays.

Per recipe:
Calories: 3,050
Sodium: 780 mg.

Protein: 45 g.
Fat: 208 g.
Carbohydrate: 499 g.

Far left: Cream Cheese Cookies, recipe page 79
Middle: Nut Cookies, recipe page 80
Far right: Pumpkin Date Cookies, recipe page 81
Top right: Parsnip Bake, recipe page 46

1 pound butter or margarine
2 cups sugar
1 teaspoon vanilla extract
10 eggs
4 cups flour
½ teaspoon salt

1 teaspoon baking powder
1 pound pitted cherries
½ pound crushed pineapple, canned
1 pound white raisins
1 pound walnuts, chopped

Preheat oven to 300°F. Beat butter or margarine, sugar, vanilla, and eggs in mixer. Sift together flour, salt, and baking powder, and add to creamed ingredients, continuing to mix. If you cannot find fresh cherries substitute equal weight of candied, sold during the holiday season. Mix in fruits and nuts by hand. Bake in 2 greased loaf pans for 2 hours.

One for your family's Christmas; one for a gift!

Makes 2

Per recipe:
Calories: 5,390
Sodium: 3,300 mg.

Protein: 75 g.
Fat: 357 g.
Carbohydrate: 468 g.

HALLOWEEN PIE

11-inch prebaked pie crust
2 envelopes unflavored
    gelatin
1½ cups milk
6 eggs, separated
½ cup sugar

12-ounce can defrosted
    orange juice concentrate
1 cup heavy cream
8-ounce bar sweet chocolate,
    shaved

Soften gelatin in ½ cup hot water. In double boiler, scald milk. Mix egg yolks with ¼ cup of the sugar. Add about ½ cup of the hot milk and return yolk mixture to rest of milk. Stir and cook slowly a few minutes until slightly thickened, taking care that mixture does not boil which would cause the eggs to scramble. Remove from heat and stir in gelatin. Blend in orange juice and chill until partially set. Beat the egg whites with remaining ¼ cup of sugar until soft peaks form. Fold in partially thickened gelatin. Whip heavy cream until peaks form. Fold into gelatin-egg mixture. Spread ⅓ of this mixture into pie crust. Sprinkle with ⅓ of chocolate shavings. Repeat. Decorate top with last ⅓ chocolate shavings by outlining a pumpkin picture or any other that takes your fancy.

Nutrition Note: Surely a higher-quality accompaniment to holiday celebration than sugar-laden marshmallow pumpkins or candy corn.

Per serving (¹⁄₁₀ pie):
Calories: 572
Sodium: 450 mg.

Protein: 13 g.
Fat: 34 g.
Carbohydrate: 54 g.

¼ cup shortening	2 cups flour
½ cup sugar	1 teaspoon salt
2 egg yolks	1 teaspoon baking soda
1 cup honey	1 cup milk

Preheat oven to 325 °F. Melt shortening and stir in sugar. Mix the yolks with the honey and stir into the shortening. Cool. Sift dry ingredients, add milk, and then combine with remaining ingredients. Stir. Pour into a large greased loaf pan and bake 1 hour.

Per recipe:	Protein: 42 g.
Calories: 3,440	Fat: 76 g.
Sodium: 2,700 mg.	Carbohydrate: 647 g.

PEACH PIE

6 ripe peaches	Pinch of salt
Whole Wheat Crumb Crust	1 cup milk
(see p. 125)	2 eggs, beaten
¾ cup sugar	¼ teaspoon almond extract
1 tablespoon flour	

Preheat oven to 400 °F. Peel peaches, cut in halves, and remove stones. Arrange them cut side up in the pie shell. Mix sugar, flour, and salt. Stir in milk, eggs, and almond extract. Pour over peaches and bake in 400 °F oven for 10 minutes. Reduce heat to 325 °F, and continue baking 40–50 minutes until custard is firm.

Per serving (⅛ pie):	Protein: 7 g.
Calories: 325	Fat: 11 g.
Sodium: 205 mg.	Carbohydrate: 48 g.

PLUM CAKE

½ cup shortening
1 cup sugar
2 eggs
2 cups flour

2 teaspoons baking powder
¾ cup milk
1 teaspoon vanilla extract
3 pounds purple plums

Topping:

½ pint sour cream
1 teaspoon vanilla extract

2 tablespoons confectioner's
sugar

Preheat oven to 350°F. In mixer, cream together shortening, sugar, and eggs. Sift together flour and baking powder and add to creamed ingredients, alternating with milk and vanilla as the mixer continues to operate. Pour batter into a greased 13x9-inch pan. Cut the plums in half and pit, overlapping them skin side up over the batter. Bake 45 minutes. Mix together topping ingredients and spread over baked cake after it has cooled.

Nutrition Note: The plums add an unusual touch and contribute vitamin A and potassium. Has the natural taste of Christmas subtly baked in.

Per recipe:
Calories: 4,000
Sodium: 2,000 mg.

Protein: 63 g.
Fat: 138 g.
Carbohydrate: 630 g.

Left: Pumpkin Cake, recipe page 105

Whole Wheat Crumb Crust
  (see p. 125)
1 cup pumpkin, canned
  and pureed
3 eggs, separated
½ cup sugar
1 cup milk
½ teaspoon salt
½ teaspoon ground allspice

¼ teaspoon nutmeg
1 teaspoon cinnamon
2 tablespoons margarine,
  melted
1 tablespoon unflavored
  gelatin
¼ cup cold water
½ cup sugar
1 cup heavy cream, whipped

Preheat oven to 350°F. and bake crust 10–12 minutes. Cook pumpkin in a double boiler 10 minutes. Mix egg yolks, sugar, and milk, and add to pumpkin. Add salt, spices, and margarine. Cook slowly, stirring, until of custard consistency. Do not allow mixture to boil. Remove from heat. Soften gelatin in cold water until dissolved. Add to pumpkin. Chill. Beat egg whites, adding 1/2 cup sugar until stiff and peaky. Fold into pumpkin mix and pour into baked crumb crust. Top with whipped cream.

Per serving (⅒ slice):
Calories: 350
Sodium: 300 mg.

Protein: 7 g.
Fat: 21 g.
Carbohydrate: 33 g.

PUMPKIN CAKE

½ cup margarine or butter
1 cup brown sugar
2 eggs
¾ cup canned pumpkin
1¾ cups flour
1 teaspoon soda

1 teaspoon cinnamon
½ teaspoon salt
½ teaspoon nutmeg
¼ teaspoon ginger
¼ teaspoon ground cloves
¾ cup chopped nuts

Topping:

½ cup confectioner's sugar
⅛ teaspoon nutmeg

⅛ teaspoon cinnamon
2 tablespoons heavy cream

Preheat oven to 350°F. Cream together margarine or butter, sugar, and eggs, and then add pumpkin. Thoroughly blend dry ingredients except nuts, stir into pumpkin mixture. Stir in nuts. Bake in a greased 2-quart pan for 65–75 minutes. Blend topping ingredients to a glazy consistency and spread on slightly cooled cake. Let stand several hours before slicing.

Per recipe:
Calories: 3,630
Sodium: 1,600 mg.

Protein: 42 g.
Fat: 115 g.
Carbohydrate: 606 g.

RAISIN CAKE

1 pound raisins	1 teaspoon salt
½ cup shortening	2 cups water
2 cups sugar	3 cups whole wheat flour
1 teaspoon cinnamon	1 teaspoon baking soda

Preheat oven to 325°F. Simmer raisins, shortening, sugar, cinnamon, and salt in the water for 5 minutes. Cool. Add flour and baking soda. Pour into greased 9x13-inch pan and bake for 1 hour.

Nutrition Note: Where there are raisins, there are iron, potassium, and dietary fiber, and where there is whole wheat flour, there are B vitamins.

Per recipe:
Calories: 5,100
Sodium: 2,700 mg.

Protein: 55 g.
Fat: 109 g.
Carbohydrate: 975 g.

1 cup milk
1 teaspoon vanilla
2 eggs
⅓ cup honey
2 cups cooked brown
  rice

1 cup raisins or chopped
  dates
½ teaspoon each cinnamon,
  lemon rind
Dash nutmeg
1 cup plain yogurt

Combine milk and vanilla. Mix eggs and honey together and blend with milk. Add rice, raisins or dates, cinnamon, lemon rind, and nutmeg. Pour mixture into a buttered 1-quart casserole and bake in a 350°F oven for 25 to 30 minutes, stirring every 10 minutes. Remove from oven and let cool and thicken. After 10 or 15 minutes, stir in yogurt.

Serves 5

Nutrition Note: So rich in vitamins, minerals, and the basics of healthy eating.

Per serving:
Calories: 325
Sodium: 225 mg.

Protein: 8 g.
Fat: 6 g.
Carbohydrate: 59 g.

CHEESE BALLS

1½–2 pounds Cheddar cheese	⅛ teaspoon garlic salt
½ pound margarine	8 ounces cream cheese
½ small onion, minced	1 cup chopped walnuts

Melt Cheddar and margarine together in a double boiler. Add minced onion and garlic salt to taste. With a beater, whip the cream cheese into the warm Cheddar mixture until smooth. Chill overnight in refrigerator. Next day (at least 20 hours later) form into small balls and roll in chopped nuts.

Serves 24

Nutrition Note: Kick the sugar habit. Try these for after-school snacks.

Per serving:	Protein: 10 g.
Calories: 270	Fat: 25 g.
Sodium: 375 mg.	Carbohydrate: 2 g.

DATE BALLS

½ cup margarine	1 tablespoon milk
¾ cup sugar	½ teaspoon salt
8-ounce package dates, chopped	½ cup nuts, chopped
1 egg, beaten	2 cups Rice Krispies
1 teaspoon vanilla extract	Toasted coconut or chopped walnuts

Melt margarine and add sugar and dates, simmering until it reaches a boil. Beat together the egg, vanilla, milk, and salt. Add to date mixture, while still simmering slowly. Cool. Add nuts and Rice Krispies. Form into balls about the size of a walnut and roll in coconut or walnuts. Place on a sheet of waxed paper and refrigerate.

Makes about 48

Nutrition Note: Move over candy, these delicious date balls will satisfy any sweet tooth and satisfy our needs for iron, potassium, and fiber as well.

Per serving:	Protein: 0.5 g.
Calories: 65	Fat: 3 g.
Sodium: 70 mg.	Carbohydrate: 8 g.

½ cup granola
½ cup wheat germ
½ cup dried skim milk
¼ cup brown sugar
⅛ teaspoon salt
½ cup sesame seeds or
   sunflower seeds

½ cup raisins or
   chopped dried fruit
1½ cups crunchy peanut
   butter (approximately)
1 cup unsweetened dry
   coconut

Mix all ingredients except peanut butter and coconut. Then add enough of the peanut butter to make the mixture stiff but not crumbly. Roll into bite-size balls, and roll the balls in the shredded coconut. Chill in covered dish in refrigerator.

Pop these into the lunchbox sandwich bag, covered with wax paper, for an energy-packed dessert.

3 dozen

Per serving:
Calories: 120
Sodium: 30 mg.

Protein: 5 g.
Fat: 7 g.
Carbohydrate: 9 g.

CREAMED FRUIT

1 lemon
2 cups ricotta cheese
1 egg yolk
1 tablespoon melted butter or
  margarine
⅛ teaspoon salt

2 tablespoons honey
Mixed fresh fruits
  (sliced banana, apple,
  orange, tangerine, grapes,
  cherries, berries, etc.)

Wash and grate rind from lemon. Squeeze juice from lemon. Whip all ingredients except fruit with a whisk and pour mixture over fruit.

Makes 2 cups

Nutrition Note: An elegant yet simple fruit topping that is more than a syrupy sauce or heavy cream. Ricotta cheese is rich in protein and calcium, and the fruit is rich in natural vitamin C.

Per serving (½ cup):
Calories: 260
Sodium: 625 mg.

Protein: 15 g.
Fat: 99 g.
Carbohydrate: 28 g.

FRUIT AND YOGURT TREAT

½ cup raisins
2 apples, peeled and cored
½ cup water
1 small box strawberries

1 tablespoon honey
3 cups plain yogurt
½ cup chopped nuts

Simmer raisins and apples in water until soft. Cool and add half of the strawberries, the honey, and 1 cup of the yogurt. Puree in blender. Slice remaining strawberries and stir through mixture. In dessert dishes, spoon portions of remaining yogurt on bottom, top with fruit-yogurt mixture, and garnish with chopped nuts.

Serves 6

Nutrition Note: Goodbye ice cream, hello Fruit and Yogurt Treat …and hello fewer calories, less sugar, and vitamin C.

Per serving:
Calories: 240
Sodium: 70 mg.

Protein: 5 g.
Fat: 11 g.
Carbohydrate: 31 g.

Combine any of the following: Berries
Tangerine sections   Grapes
Banana slices   Sour cream or plain yogurt,
Pear slices   sweetened with honey to
Apple slices   taste

Top fruit with sweetened sour cream or yogurt.

Per serving (1 cup):   Protein: 7 g.
Calories: 230   Fat: 8 g.
Sodium: 125 mg.   Carbohydrate: 32 g.

Right: Custard, recipe page 98

CINNAMON PEACHES

2 large cans of peach halves	1 stick cinnamon
1 orange, thinly sliced	4 whole cloves
½ cup brown sugar	1 teaspoon ground allspice
⅓ cup vinegar	

Drain peaches into a saucepan and set fruit aside. Add remaining ingredients to juice in pan and simmer 10 minutes. Add peaches and simmer 5 minutes more. Cool and refrigerate in covered jar.

Keep a jar of these pickled peaches on hand to serve in small dishes with lunch.

Per serving:
Calories: 150
Sodium: 10 mg.

Protein: 0.5 g.
Fat: 0 g.
Carbohydrate: 37 g.

Right: Eggnog, recipe page 12

Clean, cut up, wash, and drain any combination of the following:

Carrot sticks   Raw broccoli flowerettes,
Celery sticks   bite-size
Raw cauliflowerettes,   Cucumber sticks
   bite-size   Radishes

Dip

Mix any needed quantity, in this ratio: 1 pint sour cream, 1
envelope dry onion soup.

Per recipe: Protein: 21 g.
Calories: 435   Fat: 21 g.
Sodium: 3,600 mg.   Carbohydrate: 41 g.

RED AND WHITE FROSTIES

1-pound can jellied cranberry   ¼ cup mayonnaise
   sauce   ¼ cup confectioner's sugar,
3 tablespoons lemon juice   sifted
1 package paper cups   1 cup walnuts, chopped
3 ounces cream cheese,   1 cup heavy cream, whipped
   softened

Crush the cranberry sauce with a fork and add the lemon juice.
Half fill paper cups with this mixture. Combine cream cheese,
mayonnaise, and sugar. Add walnuts. Whip the cream and fold in
the cheese mix. Spoon this mixture over the cranberry mix.
Freeze. When ready to use, split the paper cups gently and peel
away, or soften their sides by running hot water briefly over
them. You can also make an ice-pop out of these ices by putting
a stick in before freezing.

Makes 12–24, depending on size of paper cups

Per serving: Protein: 2 g.
Calories: 270   Fat: 20 g.
Sodium: 50 mg.   Carbohydrate: 20 g.

STICKS AND STONES

2 cups Wheat Chex
2 cups small pretzel sticks
1 cup Rice Chex
1 cup coconut chips
8 ounces walnuts
12 ounces pecans
3½ ounces popcorn kernels, popped

½ pound melted margarine
½ teaspoon garlic salt
1 teaspoon salt
1 teaspoon curry powder
1 tablespoon Worcestershire sauce
1 clove garlic, peeled

Preheat oven to 250°F. Blend together first 7 ingredients. Mix melted margarine, seasonings, and Worcestershire thoroughly and sprinkle over dry mixture. Toss in the garlic clove. Bake 1 hour in a large roasting pan, stirring occasionally. Remove garlic clove and allow mixture to cool before storing.

Store in plastic bags with wire ties for a snack that will either be on hand for a few weeks at home or feed a classroom full of kids all at once.

Makes 4 or 5 large bowlfuls

Nutrition Note: Far and away a smarter nutritional buy than chips.

Per recipe:
Calories: 5,500
Sodium: 7,850 mg.

Protein: 75 g.
Fat: 445 g.
Carbohydrate: 300 g.

1 box of pitted dates
1 cup peanut butter
1 cup walnuts

1 cup confectioner's or
   granulated sugar (optional)

Stuff the dates with peanut butter and push a walnut into the stuffing. Roll dates in sugar.

This makes a nice Christmas treat.

Nutrition Note: Though rich in calories, each date is stuffed with protein, iron, potassium, and fiber.

Per serving:
Calories: 68
Sodium: 4 mg.

Protein: 1 g.
Fat: 4 g.
Carbohydrate: 7 g.

FROZEN FRUIT

Cut a banana in half, push a Popsicle stick into the flat side, roll in wheat germ and freeze. Wash green seedless grapes and dip in sugar. Freeze.

Nutrition Note: What a wonderful habit to get into!

Per serving:	banana (wheat germ)	grapes (sugar)
Calories:	105	300
Sodium:	trace	trace
Protein:	5 g.	2 g.
Fat:	1 g.	0 g.
Carbohydrate:	20 g.	73 g.

SUPER C POPSICLE

1 banana
⅓ cup honey
6-ounce can orange juice concentrate, thawed

10-ounce package frozen strawberries, thawed
2 cups apple juice

Mix all ingredients together in a blender. Pour into paper cups. Freeze. Insert a Popsicle stick when half frozen.

Note: Any berries can be substituted for the strawberries.

Makes 10–20, depending on size of paper cups.

Per serving (1 pop):
Calories: 65
Sodium: 2 mg.

Protein: 0 g.
Fat: 0 g.
Carbohydrate: 16 g.

Package of small paper cups   Popsicle sticks
Any kind of fruit juice

Freeze paper cups full of fruit juice, inserting sticks when consistency is strong enough to keep them upright. When you use
these, peel paper off and munch like an ice-pop!

Nutrition Note: When the ice cream truck comes down the block,
bring out these vitamin-rich pops.

Per serving (3-ounce pop):   Protein: 0 g.
Calories: 65   Fat: 0 g.
Sodium: 5 mg.   Carbohydrate: 16 g.

LASSI TO GO

½ cup buttermilk   ½ cup favorite fruit juice

You don't even need the blender for this! Combine ingredients,
drink, and enjoy.

Nutrition Note: Look out powdered fruit drinks, watch out soda
pop, this alternative features no added sugar, lots of vitamins,
minerals, and even some protein!

Per serving (1 cup):   Protein: 4 g.
Calories: 110   Fat: 0 g.
Sodium: 165 mg.   Carbohydrate: 23 g.

FRUIT MILK DRINKS (FOR LOTS OF KIDS)

To a basic mixture of:
1 cup cold water
¼ cup dry milk
1 tablespoon honey

Add:
⅓ cup frozen juice
concentrate

Adjust amount of honey to taste, depending on the juice.

Per serving (1 cup):
Calories: 85
Sodium: 80 mg.

Protein: 5 g.
Fat: trace
Carbohydrate: 16 g.

YOGURT DRINK

1 cup frozen juice
concentrate

1 cup plain yogurt
3 cups water

Blend. Just about any juice can be used according to the ratio 1-1-3.

6 glasses

Nutrition Note: The benefits speak for themselves: protein, calcium, and the vitamins natural to fruit juice. If a meal has been skipped or missed in the course of a day, here's a wonderfully refreshing way to supplement one's daily requirements.

Per serving (1 cup):
Calories: 85
Sodium: 20 mg.

Protein: 2 g.
Fat: 2 g.
Carbohydrate: 15 g.

Combine a scoop of vanilla ice cream with 1 cup of your favorite juice and blend. Especially good with: Grape juice; Apple juice; Lemon-lime juice; Pineapple juice; Apricot nectar.

Nutrition Note: Once they try this version of a float, they'll be hooked—but that's just fine in this case.

Per serving (1 cup):   Protein: 2 g.
Calories: 185   Fat: 6 g.
Sodium: 40 mg.   Carbohydrate: 30 g.

Bottom, right: Nut Cookies, recipe page 80

12-ounce can tomato paste ⅛ teaspoon cumin
½ cup vinegar ⅛ teaspoon nutmeg
½ cup water ⅛ teaspoon pepper
½ teaspoon salt ½ teaspoon mustard
1 teaspoon oregano

Combine ingredients and store in refrigerator. Make your own and don't worry about preservatives!

Makes 2½ cups

Per recipe: Protein: 12 g.
Calories: 329 Fat: 1 g.
Sodium: 1,330 mg. Carbohydrate: 68 g.

HOMEMADE MAYONNAISE

1 egg 2 tablespoons cider vinegar
½ teaspoon salt 1 cup oil
½ teaspoon mustard powder

Put first 4 ingredients in a blender with 1 tablespoon of the oil. Blend on medium speed, uncovered, very slowly adding the rest of the oil. Adding too much oil at a time can cause curdling. If this should happen to your sauce, pour it out of the blender, put another egg in the blender, and slowly turn on again while pouring curdled sauce back in.

Makes 1¼ cups

Per recipe: Protein: 7 g.
Calories: 2,050 Fat: 224 g.
Sodium: 1,250 mg. Carbohydrate: 2 g.

¾ cup whole wheat bread
  crumbs (shred dry bread
  in blender)
¼ cup powdered skim milk
¾ teaspoon cinnamon

¼ cup granola
¼ cup melted butter or
  margarine
2 teaspoons honey

Mix together and flatten against bottom and sides of a greased pie plate. This can be used as an alternative to pastry crust.

Makes 2 cups

Nutrition Note: A delightfully healthy alternative to the usual "white" flour-and-shortening crust.

Per recipe:
Calories: 1,170
Sodium: 1,150 mg.

Protein: 38 g.
Fat: 70 g.
Carbohydrate: 98 g.

WHOLE WHEAT PIE CRUST

1½ cups whole wheat flour
  or combination of same with
  whole wheat pastry flour
½ cup wheat germ

1 teaspoon salt
10 tablespoons margarine
4–6 tablespoons cold water

Stir dry ingredients together. Cut margarine into flour mixture with knives or pastry cutter. When the dough is the consistency of rolled oats, sprinkle with water enough to hold together. The dough is easier to roll if chilled beforehand for at least ½ hour. Roll out on lightly floured surface or between sheets of waxed paper with rolling pin.

Makes 1 10-inch bottom crust or 1 8-inch bottom crust with lattice strips

Per recipe:
Calories: 1,960
Sodium: 3,700 mg.

Protein: 45 g.
Fat: 123 g.
Carbohydrate: 169 g.

Blueberry Cream Pie, recipe page 93

BASIC ITALIAN TOMATO SAUCE

2 tablespoons olive oil
1 cup chopped onion
2 garlic cloves, minced
2 green peppers, chopped
2 teaspoons basil
1 teaspoon oregano
2 bay leaves
1 teaspoon salt

2 medium fresh tomatoes, chopped
6 ounces tomato paste
29-ounce can tomato puree
2 tablespoons dry wine
½ teaspoon black pepper
½ cup fresh parsley, chopped
½ cup grated Parmesan cheese

Sauté first 8 ingredients in a large saucepan or dutch oven until onions are limp. Add tomatoes, paste, puree, wine, and pepper. Turn heat to low. Cover and simmer 45 minutes to 1 hour, stirring occasionally. Add parsley and cheese.

Makes 2 quarts

	per recipe (2 quarts)	per serving (1 cup)
Calories:	1,070	135
Sodium:	5,900 mg.	700 mg.
Protein:	41 g.	5 g.
Fat:	40 g.	5 g.
Carbohydrate:	136 g.	17 g.

CRUNCHY COATING MIX

⅔ cup yellow cornmeal
½ cup grated Parmesan cheese
⅓ cup sesame seeds
⅓ cup wheat germ
4 teaspoons parsley flakes

4 teaspoons garlic powder
1 tablespoon thyme leaves
2 teaspoons sage
1 teaspoon salt
1 teaspoon pepper

Shake ingredients together in a large plastic bag. Close tightly with a wire tie and store in refrigerator to use as a poultry breading over beaten egg dip.

Makes about 2½ cups

Per recipe:
Calories: 1,510
Sodium: 2,400 mg.

Protein: 68 g.
Fat: 76 g.
Carbohydrate: 140 g.

½ cup mayonnaise   1 tablespoon lemon juice
½ cup plain yogurt   ¼ teaspoon salt
½ cup crumbled blue cheese   Few drops of Tabasco

Blend together and serve on tossed salad.

Per recipe: Protein: 28 g.
Calories: 1,440   Fat: 144 g.
Sodium: 1,300 mg.   Carbohydrate: 8 g.

HERB DRESSING

½ cup olive oil   1 tablespoon chopped parsley
2 tablespoons vinegar   1 teaspoon lemon juice
1 teaspoon salt   Few drops Worcestershire
½ teaspoon pepper   sauce
1 teaspoon marjoram

Combine and blend. Chill, and reblend before using.

Per recipe: Protein: 0 g.
Calories: 965   Fat: 105 g.
Sodium: 2,300 mg.   Carbohydrate: 5 g.

THOUSAND ISLAND DRESSING

1 cup mayonnaise	Dash of salt
½ cup chili sauce	2 hard-boiled eggs,
⅓ cup drained pickle relish	coarsely chopped

Mix thoroughly and chill before using.

Per recipe:	Protein: 20 g.
Calories: 2,025	Fat: 185 g.
Sodium: 2,450 mg.	Carbohydrate: 70 g.

VINAIGRETTE DRESSING

½ cup oil	1 teaspoon dry mustard or
3 tablespoons wine vinegar	Dijon mustard
1 teaspoon salt	½ teaspoon basil
Freshly ground pepper	Pinch thyme, or other favorite
to taste	herb to taste

Blend well before pouring over cold vegetables or salad.

Per recipe:	Protein: 1 g.
Calories: 990	Fat: 108 g.
Sodium: 2,500 mg.	Carbohydrate: 4 g.